Caring for Children through Crochet

A Prayer Shawl Ministry Handbook

EVELYN RAINEY

Copyright © 2023 by Evelyn Rainey
Photographs © 2023 Evelyn Rainey
Cover Design © 2023 by Evelyn Rainey

All rights reserved. No part of this book may be reproduced, scanned, or distributed in any printed, audio or electronic form **without permission**. (Contact the author for permission.) Such piracy of copyrighted materials is a violation of the author's rights and is punishable by law.

Paper back ISBN-13: 978-1-946469-70-0
Hardcover ISBN-13: 978-1-946469-71-7

ShelteringTree.Earth, LLC Publishing
PO Box 973, Eagle Lake, FL 33839

Did you enjoy this book?
We love to hear from our readers.
Please visit the author at
ShelteringTree.Earth

About the Cover:
Clarice Kidd loves her dragon cape.

CARING FOR CHILDREN THROUGH CROCHET

DEDICATION

To all my students –
academic, crochet, Sunday School, and writing.

With Grateful Appreciation
To the members of the
United Methodist Temple Prayer Shawl Ministry: Caryl Kelley, Beverly Powell, Diane Poling, Judy Shively, Trish Spurlin, and Loiuse Urquhart, and especially to Pastor Pam DeDea, who supported the idea of starting a PSM at the church.

CARING FOR CHILDREN THROUGH CROCHET

CONTENTS

Foreword	i
Matthew 25:34-40	1
Psalm 90:16	3
Beginner's How-To Crochet	4
Psalm 103:17-18	18
Easy Cap Pattern	20
Psalm 127:3	24
The Needs Of Adoptive Parents And Children	25
Psalm 127:4-5	28
Kimono	29
Psalm 131:2	41
Diaper Cover	42
Proverbs 22:6	44
Ministering To Gifted Children and Parents	46
Isaiah 49:15	53
Baby Booties	55
Isaiah 9:5	61
Basic Ripple Afghan	63
2 Chronicles 20:13, 31:18	74
Ministering To Children and Parents with Special Needs	76
Joshua 14:9	79

Breast-Feeding Modesty Shawl	80
Deuteronomy 31:12	98
Button Covers	99
Deuteronomy 28:4	106
Parenting as a Ministry	108
Deuteronomy 4:40	112
Crocheted Egg Rattles	114
Matthew 2:11	118
Finger Puppets	120
Matthew 7:11; Luke 11:13	127
Ministering To New Parents And Grandparents	129
John 16:21	133
Scarf	135
Matthew 19:13-14; Mark 10:13-15; Luke 18:16-17	139
Mittens	141
Matthew 18:2-5; Mark 9:36-37	149
The Innocent Bystanders of Domestic Violence / Intimate Partner Violence Exposure	152
Acts 2:39	158
Crocheted Plastic Hangers	159
I Thessalonians 2:5-8	162
Huggable Toys	164
1 John 3:1-2	175

Ministering To Children Through Crochet	177
I John 3:18	180
Dragon Cape	181
1 John 5:2	188
3 John 1:4	189
The Benediction	190
About Creative Crochet Patterns	191
About The Author	195
About Shelteringtree.Earth	197

FOREWORD

Every year, I would post this anonymous poem in my classroom and send a copy home to parents:

Children Learn What They Live

If a child lives with criticism,
He learns to condemn.
If a child lives with hostility,
He learns to fight.
If a child lives with ridicule,
He learns to be shy.

If a child lives with tolerance,
He learns to be patient.
If a child lives with encouragement,
He learns confidence.
If a child lives with praise,
He learns to appreciate.

If a child lives with fairness,
He learns justice.
If a child lives with security,
He learns faith.
If a child lives with approval,
He learns to like himself.

If a child lives with acceptance and friendship,
He learns to find love in the world.

Author Unknown

MATTHEW 25:34-40

³⁴ Then the King will say to those on His right, 'Come, you who are blessed by My Father, inherit the kingdom prepared for you from the foundation of the world. ³⁵ For I was hungry and you gave Me something to eat; I was thirsty and you gave Me something to drink; I was a stranger and you invited Me in; ³⁶ I was naked and you clothed Me; I was sick and you visited Me; I was in prison and you came to Me.'
³⁷ "Then the righteous will answer Him, 'Lord, when did we see You hungry and feed You? Or thirsty and give You something to drink? ³⁸ And when did we see You a stranger and invite You in? Or naked and clothe You? ³⁹ When did we see You sick, or in prison, and come to You?'
⁴⁰ "And answering, the King will say to them, 'Amen, I tell you, whatever you did to one of the least of these My brethren, you did it to Me.'[1]

---

[1] All Scripture in this book is taken from the Tree of Life (TLV) Translation of the Bible. Copyright © 2015 by The Messianic Jewish Family Bible Society.

A ministry has the needs of others as its heart. This ministry – caring for children through crochet – has Scriptures which mention children. The Lectio Davinas after each one do not address children, they address parents and how parents raise their children. Placed between these are crochet patterns for children's items you can make to keep, give away, or sell. Also evenly spaced through the book are articles written by people who work in special areas; they give advice about how any ministry can help parents and children who are in need.

How we treat our children says more about us than any technological marvel or industrial innovation. Do we feed them, and if so, with what? Do we help slake their thirst for knowledge and understanding? Do we love them even if they become strangers to us? Do we clothe them in righteousness or let them dress themselves? Do we care for them no matter what ails them? Do we go out of our way to find them when they are in a place where they cannot come to us?

It is my prayer that this book will help us feed, clothe, comfort, and heal children.

PSALM 90:16

*Let Your work appear to Your servants,
and Your splendor on their children.*

Remember the first time you saw snow and made your first snow angel? Or the first time you saw a double rainbow? What wonders! As children, the works of God are awe-inspiring and that joy stays with us as adults, so much so, we usually find ways to share those experiences with our children.

When was the last time you sat outside at night to watch the meteor showers? Are there still fireflies where you live? How about something as indomitable as a daisy growing up through a crack in the sidewalk?

Take time to point out these things to children. Let them see the majesty of God through His works.

BEGINNER'S HOW-TO CROCHET

Chain – With one loop on your hook, yarn-over, pull the yarn through the loop. You now have one (new) loop on the hook.

Slip Stitch – SS - With one loop on your hook, put your hook through the loop in the row below. You now have two loops on the hook. Yarn over and pull through both loops. You now have one (new) loop on the hook.

Single Crochet – SC - With one loop on your hook, put your hook through the loop in the row below. You now have two loops on the hook.. Yarn-over and pull through one loop. You again have 2 loops on your hook. Yarn over and pull through both loops. You now have one (new) loop on the hook.

Half-Double Crochet – HDC - With one loop on your hook, yarn-over and put your hook through the loop in the row below. You now have 3 loops on the hook. Yarn-over and pull through one loop. You again have 3 loops on your hook. Yarn over and pull through all 3 loops. You now have one (new) loop on the hook.

Double Crochet – DC - With one loop on your hook, yarn-over and put your hook through the loop in the row below. You now have 3 loops on the hook. Yarn-over and pull through one loop. You again have 3 loops on your hook. Yarn over and pull through 2 loops. You now have 2 loops on your hook. Yarn over and pull through 2 loops. You now have one (new) loop on the hook.

Triple Crochet – TC - With one loop on your hook, yarn-over twice and put your hook through the loop in the row below. You now have 4 loops on the hook. Yarn-over and pull through one loop. You again have 4 loops on your hook. Yarn over and pull through 2 loops. You now have 3 loops on your hook. Yarn over and pull through 2 loops. You now have 2 loops on your hook. Yarn over and pull through 2 loops. You now have one (new) loop on the hook.

Decrease one stitch out of two – DecSC - With one loop on your hook, put your hook through the next 2 stitches in the row below (from the front, go through both loops of the closest stitch and from the back, go through both loops of the farthest stitch). You now have 5 loops on the hook. Yarn over and pull through all 5 loops. You now have one (new) loop on the hook.

Fasten off - cut your yarn about 3 inches from your hook. Yarn-over and pull through the loop you have. Tug gently.

Practice

Work this sample in one color. Use Hook size J and weight 3 yarn. (I did the sample in a separate color for each row just to help you see the differences.)

    1.   Make a chain 10 chains long.

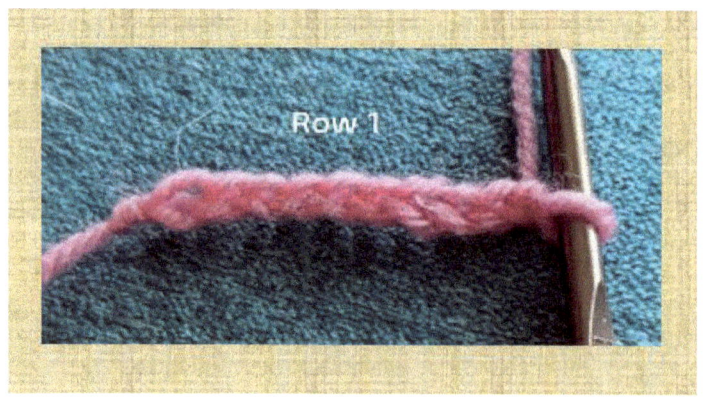

    2.   In the second chain from your hook, do one SC. Continue doing one SC in each chain until you've come to the end of your chain.

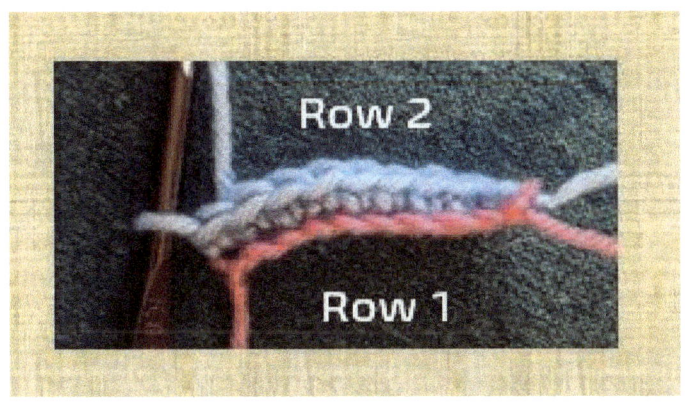

3. Chain 2. (This is called the launching chain and will have 2 chains if the rows is SC or HDC, 3 chains if the row is DC or TC.) Turn and begin working along the frontloop (the ones closest to you) of the SCs you just did. Do one HDC in the SC in the row below. Continue doing one HDC in each SC stitch from the row below until you've come to the end of your row. (Each row will have the launching chain and 8 stitches.)

4. Chain 3. Turn and begin working along the toploop of the HDCs you just did. (There are three loops on a HDC: one on the front, one above that at the top, and one in the back.) Do one DC in the DC in the row below. Continue doing one DC in each HDC stitch from the row below until you've come to the end of your row.

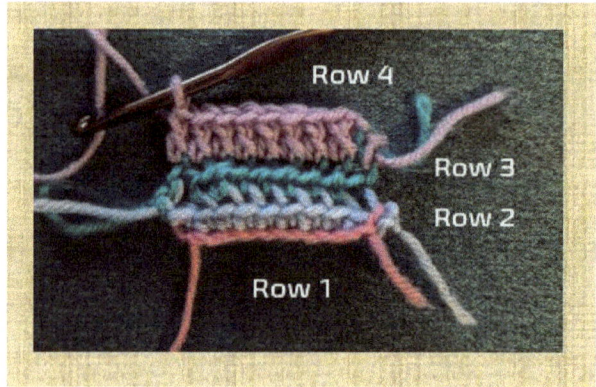

5. Chain 3. Turn and begin working along the frontloop of the DCs you just did. Do one TC in the DC in the row below. Continue doing one TC in each DC stitch from the row below until you've come to the end of your row.

6. Chain 2, turn. Do one SC in each stitch until you've come to the end of your row but put your stitch through the back loop of the stitch below. (You will need to tilt the block toward you to get to the back loop.)

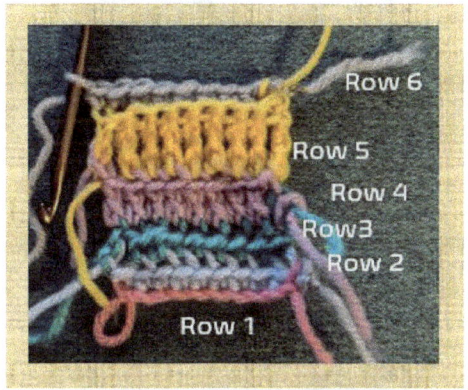

7. Chain 2, turn. Do one HDC in each stitch until you've come to the end of your row but put your stitch through the back loop of the stitch below.

8. Chain 3, turn. Do one DC in each stitch until you've come to the end of your row but put your stitch through the back loop of the stitch below.

9. Chain 3, turn. Do one TC in each stitch until you've come to the end of your row but put your stitch the back loop of the stitch below.

10. Chain 2, turn. Do one SC in each stitch until you've come to the end of your row but put your stitch through both loops of the stitch below.

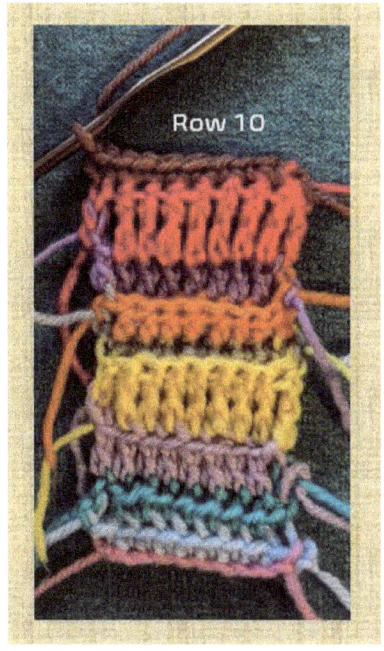

11. Chain 2, turn. Do one HDC in each stitch until you've come to the end of your row but put your stitch through both loops of the stitch below.

12. Chain 3, turn. Do one DC in each stitch until you've come to the end of your row but put your stitch through both loops of the stitch below.

13. Chain 3, turn. Do one TC in each stitch until you've come to the end of your row but put your stitch both loops of the stitch below.

14. The body of your sample is now complete, so we are going to put on a border which will be worked through both loops on the top and botton

and through the column of the stitches along the sides. Along the way, weave in any loose yarn ends if you changed colors. That means, lay the ends flat along the edge of the row and crochet over it as if it were part of the row. Each corner will have three stitches in the same loop. Chain 2 (counts as the first HDC), 2 more HDC in the same loop (the last stitch of the previous row). Rotate the sample so that you are now crocheting along the side of the rows. In row 13 (TC), crochet 3 HDC. In row 12 (DC), crochet 3 HDC. In row 11 (HDC), crochet 2 HDC. In row 10 (SC), crochet 1 HDC. In row 9 (TC), crochet 3 HDC. In row 8 (DC), crochet 3 HDC. In row 7 (HDC), crochet 2 HDC. In row 6 (SC), crochet 1 HDC. In row 5 (TC), crochet 3 HDC. In row 4 (DC), crochet 3 HDC. In row 3 (HDC), crochet 2 HDC. In row 2 (SC), crochet 1 HDC. In the first corner of the first row (the original chain), crochet 3 HDC. Rotate the sample and crochet one HDC in the loops of each stitch. That row will disappear under your border. In the last stitch, place 3 HDC. Rotate the sample and work up the side.

In row 2 (SC), crochet 1 HDC. In row 3 (HDC),

crochet 2 HDC. In row 4 (DC), crochet 3 HDC. In row 5 (TC), crochet 3 HDC. In row 6 (SC), crochet 1 HDC. In row 7 (HDC), crochet 2 HDC. In row 8 (DC), crochet 3 HDC. In row 9 (TC), crochet 3 HDC. In row 10 (SC), crochet 1 HDC. In row 11 (HDC), crochet 2 HDC. In row 12 (DC), crochet 3 HDC. In row 13 (TC), crochet 3 HDC. In the first loop of row 13, crochet 3 HDC. Rotate the sample and crochet one HDC in the loops of each stitch across the top of your sample. Slip Stitch to the first chain of this border.

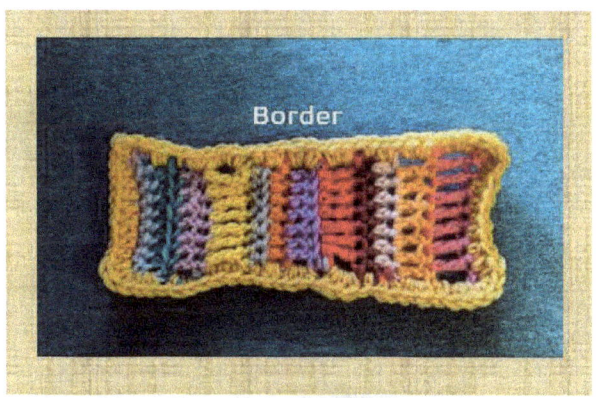

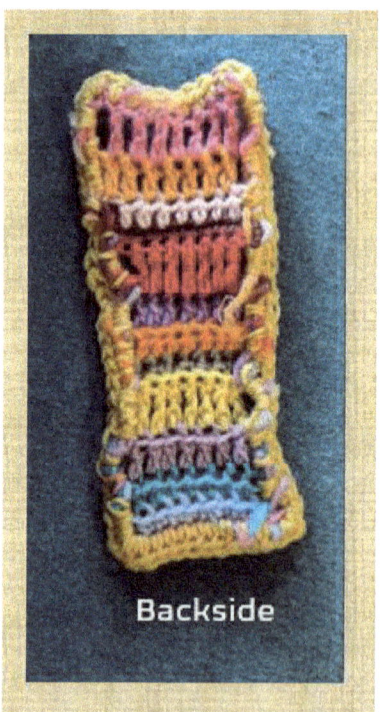

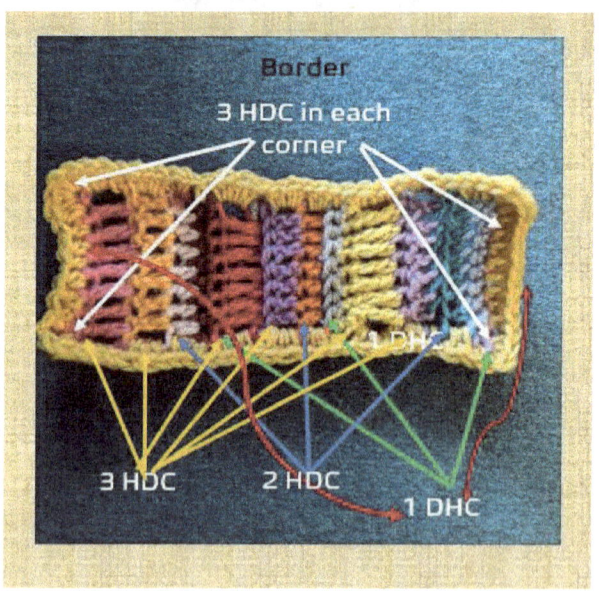

15. Fasten off. Weave in the yarn.

16. Look at your sample. Notice the height and thickness of each row, and the ridges of rows 1-9 (where you went through the front or back loop) and smoothness of 10-13 (where you went through both loops).

17. Congratulations! You are now able to do 97% of all crochet patterns available in the world!

PSALM 103:17-18

17 But the mercy of *ADONAI* is from everlasting to everlasting on those who revere Him,
His righteousness to children's children,
18 to those who keep His covenant,
who remember to observe His instructions.

How long is a *long time*? As a child, I used to think that summer lasted forever. Now, it seems that the last century was only a day or two ago. I used to tell my students that "There is no such thing as linear time." And there isn't. Time was a construct of man. The Romans from the time of Christ didn't have a concept of minutes or hours. And I'm sure you've heard the old joke comparing God's and man's grasp of the value of minutes and dimes.

God's mercy is from everlasting to everlasting, and His righteousness is not only blessed onto us but onto our children's children, as long was we keep His covenant and observe His instructions.

That's a very long time.

EASY CAP PATTERN

For teen and adult caps: J, K, M, or N sized hook. 3- or 4-ply yarn.

For infant and child caps: F or J sized hook. Baby yarn.

Crown

Chain three. Connect them in a circle. Chain two. Every time you end a row, you're going to do a slip stitch and two chains.

For the base row, put five single crochets inside the circle. Slip stitch (slip stitch means you slide the hook behind the chain-two below and grab a loop and pull it through everything on your hook). Now chain two.

For the first row, put two single crochet stitches through both loops in every stitch all the way around. Slip stitch (slide the hook behind the chain-two below and grab a loop and pull it through everything on your hook). Now chain two.

The second row, put one single crochet through both loops of the first stitch and then two single crochets through the next stitch and repeat that all the way around. One, two - five times. Slip stitch and chain two.

The next row is one single crochet twice and then two single crochets once all the way around. Pattern: One, one, two – five times.

The next row just adds another single crochet to the pattern as your circle expands outward: one single crochet three times and then two single crochets. Pattern: One, one, one, two – five times.

Then one single crochet four times and two single crochets.
Pattern: One, one, one, one, two – five times.

Then one single crochet five times and two single crochets.
Pattern: One, one, one, one, one, two – five times.

Then one single crochet six times and two single crochets.
Pattern: One, one, one, one, one, one, two – six times.

The last row of the crown is one single crochet in each stitch all the way around. Now your crown is complete.

Body of the cap
Next eighteen to twenty-four rows (your choice): The body of the cap is worked as a single crochet in each stitch, but done in the back loops. End each row with a slip stitch and chain two.

Brim
Next three rows: Double-half-crochet in both loops all the way around. End each row with a slip stitch and chain two.

For the last row, turn and single crochet through both loops all around, slip stitch and tie off. Weave the remnant yarn through the 2 chain spots.

Crochet has a rhythm to it that lends itself to scriptures, prayers and sayings. Once the crown of the cap is complete, I say the rosary along with the stitching. I'm not Catholic, but I love the rhythm and graceful words. I see nothing wrong in asking you to pray for me. In the same way, I see nothing wrong in asking Mary to pray for me. Along with the Ave Maria lines, you can repeat the Gloria Patri, the Lord's Prayer, the Apostle's Creed, and the Doxology.

Feel free to sew on flowers or bobbles. You can work these caps in solids or multicolored yarns. Stripes are fun – change the yarn at the chain-two spots. If you are keeping one color throughout the stripes, don't tie it off, just keep it waiting at the chain-2 spot until you can pick it back up again. You can also work this pattern with two threads at the same time for a much thicker cap.

Video on how to make caps for charity:

https://youtu.be/hrkf9kz7Jfs

PSALM 127:3

*Behold, children are a heritage of ADONAI
—the fruit of the womb is a reward.*

There's a difference between a gift and a reward. A gift can be something given to someone without the expectation of payment or reciprocity. It is also a natural ability, like having a gift for singing. A reward is something given to someone because of something that the recipient did.

So, is there a difference between children and the fruit of one's womb? A child is defined as a young human below the age of puberty. As written, the fruit of the womb is a baby which is the result of intense and hard labor.

So, all children are gifts from God, no matter who carried them to term or labored to birth them. We are all adopted into the kingdom of God.

THE NEEDS OF ADOPTIVE PARENTS AND CHILDREN

By Rabbi Michael Gold

My wife and I have raised three children, now young adults. We are their parents, although we have no genetic connection to them. Each was adopted at birth. Each of our children came into this world because a brave woman was willing to carry a pregnancy to term and trust us to raise her children as our own. They are adopted but they are our children.

I am aware that my children have a genetic lineage. It is part of their very being. This became clear every time their school asked them to make a family tree; "what color are your eyes and what color are your parents' eyes." Schools are not always sensitive to children raised by adoptive parents, stepparents, foster parents, or even grandparents. My children have a genetic heritage, yet we are their parents. Being a parent is not about genes but about nurturing, educating, and creating a family.

Of course, their genetic heritage is part of my children's

being. I have never kept it a secret that they are adopted. I have given them as much information as I can about their birth parents and their ethnic background. I have encouraged them to search for their birth parents when they became adults. We are white parents who raised white children. But this becomes particularly important if adopted children come from a black, Hispanic, or Asian backgrounds. We are also Jewish parents who raised three children born of non-Jewish birth mothers. Each of our children was converted to Judaism and given a strong Jewish education.

My children are aware that they are adopted. We often heard the words, "I don't have to listen to you. You are not my real parents." I would always smile and gently respond, "We are your real parents. I can show you all the legal papers to prove it." I know that parents who are raising their own biological children will often hear the words, "You are not my real parents." It is a favorite line of disobedient children.

Every human being is the product of two important factors, nature and nurture, or genetic background and upbringing. Both are important. But in our materialist age, we tend to overemphasize genes. How else can we account for the popularity of services like 23andMe. Finding one's genetic background is important. But finding and contacting long-lost biological relatives can also be disruptive and must be handled with care.

Genetics are important but in my humble opinion, upbringing is more important. The way we were raised gives us our values, our religion, our world outlook, and that network of relationships we call family. The family where a child is raised is the center of love and acceptance. Robert Frost wrote, "Home is the place where, when you have to go there, they have to take you in." My wife and I are very proud that we created a home for our three children.

About Rabbi Gold

Rabbi Michael Gold is the author of several books including *And Hanna Wept: Infertility, Adoption, and the Jewish Couple*. His most recent novel, *The Rabbi's Sex Class*, is published by ShelteringTree.Earth LLC.

He is a native of Los Angeles, CA. Rabbi Gold assumed the pulpit of Temple Beth Shalom in Boca Raton, FL in July, 2022. He is Rabbi Emeritus of Temple Beth Torah Sha'aray Tzedek in Tamarac, FL, having served the congregation 32 years. Previously he served congregations in Nyack, NY and Pittsburgh, PA.

Rabbi Gold received his PhD from Florida Atlantic University with a dissertation on process philosophy and Jewish mysticism. He is an adjunct professor of philosophy, religion, and Jewish studies at three colleges. He has lectured around the country and abroad on Jewish sexual ethics, family life, and science and spirituality Rabbi Michael and Evelyn Gold are the parents of three children and grandparents of one grandson.

PSALM 127:4-5

⁴ As arrows in the hand of a mighty man,
so are the children of one's youth.
⁵ Happy is the man whose quiver is full of them.
They will not be put to shame
when they speak with their enemies at the gate.

The thing about arrows is that they are basically useless in the quiver. They must be shot out into the world to be of use.

Letting children grow up and go on their own way is one of the hardest things a parent does. But the joy that comes from seeing your child accomplished, successful, and happy is wonderful. When you are old, you can cheerfully look back to the time your children were young and proudly to who they are as adults. Wishing for those early days to return isn't fair to you or to your children. They have become what God planned. What more could a parent ask?

KIMONO

Crochet hook size F for infant, G or J for child
Fingering yarn for infant, 3- or 4-ply sports for child
Any color or combination of colors
Buttons, snaps or ties

This sweater is an adaptation of a pattern I found in a British book. It was worked in HDC entirely. I made three of them and then got bored and started embellishing, changing the main stitch, adding this, taking that away, and trying various collars and sleeves. The instructions below will help you to do the same.

The sweater is described below in five main sections: bodice, torso, border, collar, and sleeves. Mix and match the styles to suit your needs and whims!

Colors – this sweater can be made in solid (and the first time you make it, I'd suggest you do that). If you want stripes, change the colors at the end of the row by tying off the first color and slip stitch onto that stitch after you have turned the fabric. You may also use the already striped skeins or variegated to present intriguing designs. You'll weave the ends in as you crochet the border. Trim, collar, and sleeve cuff should be the same color.

Bodice

Chain 48.

Working in your choice of loops (front loop gives a ribbed effect, both loops makes a smooth surface, etc.), one half-double crochet stitch in each stitch below unless otherwise stated

Row 1:

1 hdc in third chain from hook. 13 more hdc.

(1 hdc, chain 2, 1 hdc) in next stitch. (1 hdc, chain 2, 1 hdc) in the following stitch.

14 hdc.

(1 hdc, chain 2, 1 hdc) in next stitch. (1 hdc, chain 2, 1 hdc) in following stitch.

14 hdc. (a total of 46 HDC on this row, plus 4 chain-2 spaces)

Chain 2. Turn

Row 2:

1 hdc in each stitch below (your choice of loops) except (2 hdc, chain 2, 2 hdc) in each 2 chain space. When you reach the end of the row, chain 2, turn.

Rows 3 – 9: Repeat Row 2.

If you are going to do Tunisian sleeves, pause at this point and go down to the instructions for Tunisian Sleeves.^T

Row 10

Single crochet until you get to the first chain space. (SC in the chain space, skip all the stitches between the chain spaces, YO, put crochet hook into the 2nd chain space and YO. Draw hook back through the chain space. YO, draw through all loops on the hook.) Single crochet across to next chain space. Repeat directions in the parenthesis ( ). Single crochet across to end of the row. Chain 2, turn.

Closing the bodice under the arm.

Row 11

Double-half crochet across to under arms. Decrease the two stitches – one from each side – into one. HDC 14. Decrease two into one stitch. Continue sc until there are 15 from the next under arm. Decrease two into one stitch. SC 14, decrease the next two stitches – one from each side – into one. SC to end. Chain 2, turn. Bodice made.

Bodice Row 11

Torso

Rows 12 – 20+ (size to fit desired length)

From this point on, you can use any stitch or combination of stitches to make your pattern interesting. HDC gives a solid, warm look. DC is not as warm, works more quickly, and is softer. SC is boring, but you can do so if you wish.

If you do HDC or DC for the torso, and especially if you do fancier stitches (popcorn, shells, cross-bars, etc.), DC the first three stitches of each row and the last three of each row. Combinations make the sweater look interesting:

- ✓ Alternate rows of sc, hdc, and dc.
- ✓ Alternate stitches between sc, hdc, and dc and on the following row, match dc for the sc below and sc for the dc below, keeping the hdc the same. This gives a waffly look – very nice.
- ✓ Cross bars are really interesting. DC the first three stitches of each row and the last three of each row. So, the cross bars pattern for one row would be: 3 dc, skip one stitch, DC in next stitch –

front loop. DC in the stitch you skipped. Skip the next unworked stitch, DC front loop, DC in the stitch you skipped. Continue to the last three stitches, which you will do as DC. The rows in between these will be straight SC in back loops.

✓ Using a Tunisian crochet hook, capture all of the stitches of row 12 and do a solid Tunisian stitch for the remaining rows. This is a great base if you want to embroider or cross-stitch the torso.

I've also worked the torso in shells and popcorn clusters and any other interesting stitch you can work in a straight line. If you do fancy stitches, keep the first and the last three stitches "normal".

Border

When you make your last stitch of the torso, do not finish off unless you are changing colors.

Hdc around the outside edge.

When you get to a corner, 3 Hdc in it.

Along the sides where the stitches are perpendicular to you, put three HDC in DC, two HDC in HDC, one HDC in SC.

HDC around collar.*

Slip stitch to first HDC of the bottom row.

Finish and tie off. Weave in loose thread.

*Collar

The collar is worked as part of the trim. It can be worked these ways for various affects:

SC = collarless

HDC = Manchurian style collar

DC = collar that will fold back

TC = Ruffly collar

You can add a hood as well, but I haven't been pleased with the look.

Sleeves

Sleeves can be worked many different ways. Here are three suggestions.

From shoulder to wrist:
Start at the bottom underarm where you joined the chain spaces with the yarn-over stitches. Slip stitch to begin. HDC around. Slip stitch to first stitch, chain 2.

Continue this pattern: HDC in each stitch around, slip stitch in chain 2 space, chain 2 for each row.

Long sleeves: 9 rows of pattern or longer to match child's arm length.

Short sleeves: 3 rows of pattern.

Final row (cuff) Turn, SC around. Slip stitch to first stitch, finish off. Weave loose thread into inside of sleeve.

Or
(As attachments)
Make a rectangle of SC or HDC stitches that begins with a chain 24 (long sleeve) or 9 chain (short sleeve) and is the same number of rows as number of stitches in the armhole of your bodice. Slip stitch to join the top and bottom rows. Join with slip stitch to the y-o stitch of the bodice, slip stitch or SC along to join around the shoulder. Finish off. Weave yarn into inside of sleeve.

Or
[T] Tunisian.
Be sure that you do this style of sleeve *before* you join the front and back of the bodice under the arms.

Single crochet until you get to the first chain

space. Change your crochet hook for a Tunisian one. Do a Tunisian SC stitch through each stitch between the chain spaces. Continue the Tunisian process for fifteen rows.

Rows 16, 18, 20:

Decrease the third from the beginning and the third from the end of the row

Rows 17, 19, 21-24:

Do a Tunisian SC stitch through each stitch.
(adjust length of sleeves to fit by repeating the odd/even rows above)

Cuff: Change to a regular crochet hook. SC in each stitch for 3 rows. Turn, HDC through both loops across. With right sides together, slip stitch the two sides together, moving upward to the bodice. Don't make it too tight or the sleeve will bunch.

Single crochet until you get to the next chain space. Repeat the sleeve and the cuff directions. Single crochet until you get to the end of the row. Chain 2, return to row 11 above and then begin the torso. Don't forget to turn the sleeves right-side out.

Tunisian sleeve Row 1

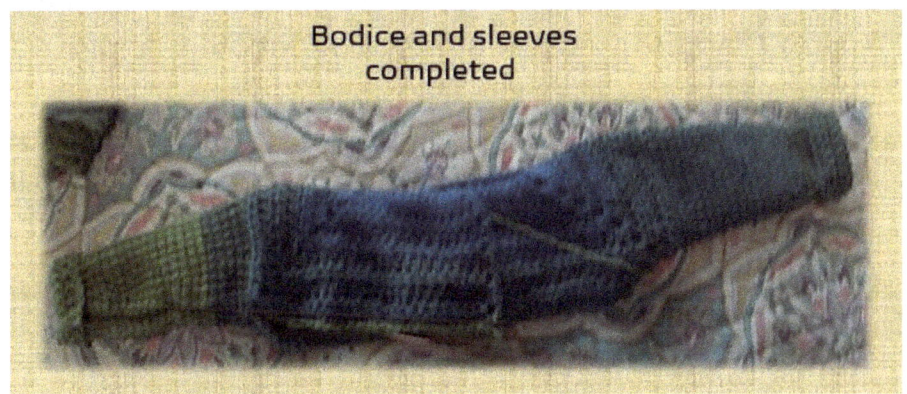

Closures

Sew buttons on at the places you want – in the center of the three plain dc along the trim. The other side of the flap will serve as a natural button hole because of the three plain dc stitches. Be careful about what buttons you choose. I've found that really bright and adorable ones often have warnings in tiny little letters that say they are not to be used for children under two. This means they most likely are a choking threat. If it states that it is not to be used by children under the age of seven, then it is most likely a lead-based paint problem. Some buttons can't be machine washed. Sew them on with more loops than you would normally do; kids love to chew on things.

Snaps are easy to sew on to the posts of the three sc borders. Again, use more thread than you would normally do for an adult garment.

Ties are fun and easy to make – just chain the number you want and sc back along it. You can attach it with a slip stitch before you begin the chain and slip stitch to finish off. Make a matching tie on the other side of the torso. Keep the ties short enough so that they won't find their ways into the baby's mouths or around their necks.

Coordinate a cap and booties with the sweater and this becomes a really nice set. Add a blanket to it and you have the perfect gift.

PSALM 131:2

But I have calmed and quieted my soul—
like a weaned child with his mother,
like a weaned child is my soul within me.

I found a small, round rocking chair when I was pregnant. I sat in it and felt it was perfectly made for me and my child. I would rock in it while pregnant and then later, as David grew, I would rock him until he fell asleep, and sing to him, rocking in tandem with the songs.

As an adult, don't you long for that feeling again – a place where all is safe and all is warm and one may find peace and rest? A place where one's soul may be quiet.

When you pray, take time to rest in God's presence. Find peace and comfort in that wonderful place of prayer.

DIAPER COVER

Yarn - 3 weight, 100% acrylic, baby colors
Crochet Hook - size G / 6 / 4.25mm
Button

You crochet this from the top down. Begin with a chain of 72.
Double Crochet every row except the border.
2 chain at beginning of each row counts as first DC.

Work 5 rows (rows 1-5) DC through both loops of each stitch. (70 stitches)

Row 6
Slip stitch 20. DC 30. Turn. Next section is only these 30 stitches.

Next 8 rows (rows 7-14):
[1 DC, DecDC 2 stitches together], then DC 11 stitches (until you get to the middle of the row). DecDC 2 stitches together. DC 11 stitches until you come within 3 stitches of the end of the row. DecDC 2 stitches together, 1 DC. Turn.

Next 8 rows (rows 15-22):
DC through both loops of each stitch. (12 stitches)

Border:
Turn with 2 chains. Single crochet around - 2 SC in each DC side, 1 SC in each DC top. 3 SC in each corner.
Slip stitch to close. Weave in tail.

Fold the diaper cover so that the middle part (that will go between the legs) comes up and the sides fold over it. Attach button to center of 3rd row of the front of the middle part. Button through DCs of flaps. As the child grows, leave the button in place, but move the flaps wider as needed.

Increase size of diaper cover by using a bigger hook.

PROVERBS 22:6

Train up a child in the way he should go,
when he is old he will not turn from it.

As a Teacher of Gifted, I met with teenagers and their parents and helped them navigate their academic hopes, expectations, and realities. I would intentionally quote this Scripture, but add at the end, "But it doesn't mention how they will behave while being a teenager." The parents all laughed, the teens mostly glowered; everyone understood that what a person does as a child and as an adult often is totally different from how they are as teenagers.

I also used to say, "Now you know why early tribes used to send their teens out on quests." The parents all looked like they were considering the option; the teens mostly glowered.

There are tough times in parents' lives when their children act like they were raised in a barn. But eventually, with a parent's nightly prayers for God's will to be done in their lives, they will remember and return to the path of love they learned from you when they were children.

MINISTERING TO GIFTED CHILDREN AND PARENTS

By Evelyn Rainey

Fifteen percent of the population – any population – is considered to have above average intelligence. These are the successful ones who make great grades and do well in their careers. And fifteen percent of any given population is also considered to have lower than average intelligence. These are the ones who need specific academic help to learn, but they can learn. But there are members of each 15% who do not fit the profile of above or below average; these make up two percent of any given population beyond the above and the below average groups. Two percent of the population is considered Gifted, and two percent of the population is considered trainable, but not educable. That leaves 70% of the world that is average. When mapped out on a graph, this is a bell-curve:

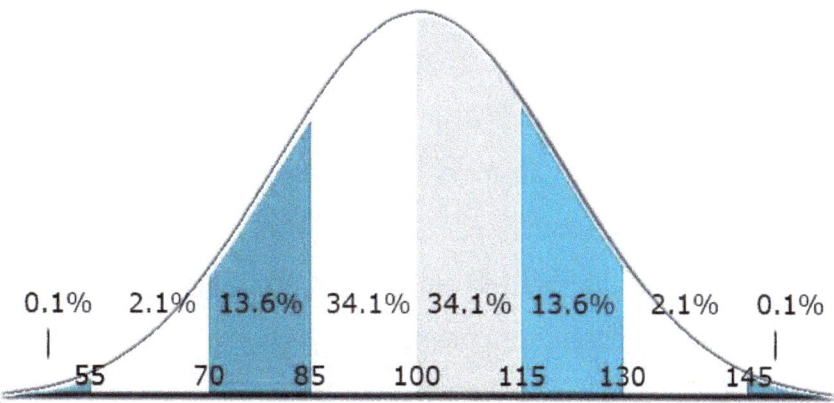

The farther ranges are not *smart* or *dumb* (although the nomenclature of Intelligence Quotience continues to slap those labels on people), but have to do with the way these individuals perceive and interact with their world. As a teacher, one is trained to identify and make accommodations to instruction and materials for these children. As a minister, one needs to realize that these children are first of all – children, but they see the world differently, and one should make accommodations to one's ministry to best meet their needs.

This article will address those who are considered Gifted. Gifted make up those two percenters and display an IQ of 130 or above. The people who rank just prior to gifted are considered above average (IQ 115-129). Above average people are those who work hard and make straight A's. Not necessarily so, the Gifted children.

Gifted people love to learn; they are voracious learners, but only if what is being taught is something that interests them.

They have horrible handwriting because their thoughts race

much faster than their hands can. Horrible handwriting is socially acceptable in doctors, but in structured classes, it is often a point of ridicule, both by peers and by teachers ("Finally, something you are not good at, and look how really bad you are at it!")

They have straight A's (because they love what you are teaching) or straight F's (because they are much more interested in learning about dinosaurs or computer games or reading a book).

They often have a severe time dealing with failure. When they were young and their peers were learning how to make mistakes and go on with their lives, Gifteds didn't make mistakes. They fooled everyone into thinking they were infallible – not intentionally, but if their parents, teachers, and peers tell them time after time that they never make mistakes, they begin to believe it. So when they actually do begin to struggle with learning (about 4th grade for boys and 9th grade for girls), they are clueless as to how to fail and keep going. They also tend to have people surrounding them pointing out this one mistake and how unusual it is (making them feel like they shouldn't make mistakes because people don't think they should.) They often deal with this strange new process one of two ways – they become perfectionists (terrified of making a mistake), or they become anarchists ("If you thought that mistake was something, look at this one!") Also, some parents take an inordinate amount of pride in their child's supposed infallibility, so once the normal path of finally finding something they are not precocious about hits, those (helicopter) parents see their child's loss of infallibility as a character flaw rather than a natural part of life.

So, learning to deal with failure is a horrible struggle which hits gifted people much later in life than the other 98% of the population.

It is at this time (if not earlier) that gifted children begin to isolate themselves from other children and their parents. They are more comfortable with non-authoritarian (or non-conforming) adults, but this causes social problems for them, too. Being made into the Teacher's Pet is one of the worst things a teacher or leader can do to a gifted child, who is already isolated from their peers as it is.

Another characteristic of Gifted people is a heightened sense of justice. They are incensed by inequalities. Their sense of right and wrong may not match that of society or religion. These are the children who shout out (oftentimes with great anguish), "It's not fair!" And the fact that most people couldn't care less if there is injustice in a situation further isolates them. They never – even as adults – seem to understand that the world is not fair and probably never will be fair. These are the children who will turn their passion into saving endangered creatures or protesting against a law or boycotting a product or business. These are also the children who discern that rules are not obeyed by or applied to everyone. Once they grasp the truth of this enigma, gifteds often learn creative and intriguing ways to circumvent said rules.

These are your leaders – where they stand in front of a group and everyone follows them. However, they may lead them into the next chapter of the lesson, or they may lead them out the door and down the hall!

Gifted children will question a lesson, commandment, or rule; it is their nature to see beyond what the 98% of the world sees. Undeniably, it is their nature to challenge what the 98% of the world unquestioningly believes. As their minister, setting ground rules and social boundaries will help, as long as you are consistent with keeping them and making sure all follow them, no matter what.

Gifted children have a deeper and greater knowledge about things and desire to share that with their friends. They are not being know-it-all's; they are sharing the bounty of what they know about the subject. As the minister, if you allow others to roll their eyes or make fun of this gift of knowledge, you are allowing that Gifted child to become further isolated from their peers, and from your religion and God. But a simple rule that limits questions and comments to the end of the lesson or to 60 seconds – and is followed consistently and fairly by all the children in the group – will go well.

Setting up groups and assigning specific roles to each member will help utilize each child's strengths – the best handwriter becomes the secretary of the group, the best reader becomes the one who reads the material aloud to the group and keeps them moving along, the one who can't sit still becomes the time-keeper and materials collector and distributor, and the Gifted student becomes the arbitrator – the one who listens to all ideas and debates the pros and cons but also is tasked to help the group achieve the goal of the activity. Praise each member in their success – and praise them with equity. This teaches that there is just as much importance in passing out the crayons as in solving the riddle. This is a lesson all children should learn (and all adults, also).

So, be consistent, be fair and just, treat each child the way you want to be treated, and accept the gift of deep and enriching knowledge each child can add to a lesson. We are all made in the image and likeness of God, even the know-it-alls and the geeks and the loners. It is your hope that they can see God in you, but it is your responsibility to see God in each of them.

Review of Gifted Characteristics:
    Voracious Learners (of educationally-acceptable or off-track knowledge)
    Leadership Qualities (for good or evil)
    Overwhelming Sense of Justice (and will hold you accountable for your actions)
    Perfectionist or Anarchist (when dealing with successes and failures)
    Horrible Handwriting (and other motor skills)

Suggestions:
Praise the good
Redirect the bad
Be consistent in all things

About Evelyn Rainey
    Evelyn has Bachelor of Science degrees in Early Childhood and Elementary Education. She also has certificates and

endorsements in English for Speakers of Other Languages, Journalism, Middle School Integrated Curriculum, and Gifted Education. She served as a Teacher of Gifted for fifteen years, traveling from school to school, teaching teachers how to successfully deal with Gifted students. These schools were traditional elementary, middle, and high schools, but also included jails (DJJ), alternative schools (for those who had been expelled but were still legally required to receive an education), and teen parent centers.

ISAIAH 49:15

Can a woman forget her nursing baby
or lack compassion for a child of her womb?
Even if these forget,
I will not forget you.

Yes, a woman can forget her children. A woman can look on the face of her daughter or son and see only a stranger. This happens every morning when I go to wake my mother, change her diapers, and administer her medications. She looks at me and smiles, but she doesn't know who I am. She doesn't remember how to form words to ask me who I am. The name she chose for me is forgotten. But she smiles. She doesn't remember who I used to be, but she knows that I take care of her. I feed her yummy puddings and tasty soft foods and hold her hand and sing with her and dress her in pretty clothes.

So, yes, a woman can forget her child, but God will never forget me. And because of that, I can show my mother unconditional love, whether she knows me or not.

BABY BOOTIES

Booties are worked in two parts: the foot and the cuff. They can be worked in any size yarn, but the smaller the hook, the smaller the bootie. Baby yarn and size f or smaller hook makes a new-born size. Three-ply yarn and size f hook makes a one-year size. In general, one skein with seven ounces of yarn will make nine pairs.

Foot:
- chain 3, join in circle

Row 1 – the medallion
- Chain 3, turn – counts as a DC, 17 DC in circle. Slip stitch to top of the chain.

Row 1 – the ruffle and around
- Ruffle: chain 3 (do not turn), using front loop for ruffle: (slip stitch, chain 3, slip stitch, chain 3) in each loop for 3 stitches. Then slip stitch, chain 3.
- Slip stitch in back loop of next stitch.
- In back loop of each individual stitch here as you work around the circle:
    - SC

- HDC
- HDC
- DC
- DC
- 2 DC in each of the next 2 stitches
- DC
- DC
- HDC
- HDC
- SC
- SC (This should put you at the ruffle.)

Row 2

- Chain 12. Attach with slip stitch at the other side of the ruffle (where you ended the last chain and began stitching around the medallion).
- SC in each stitch around medallion. DC in each chain stitch

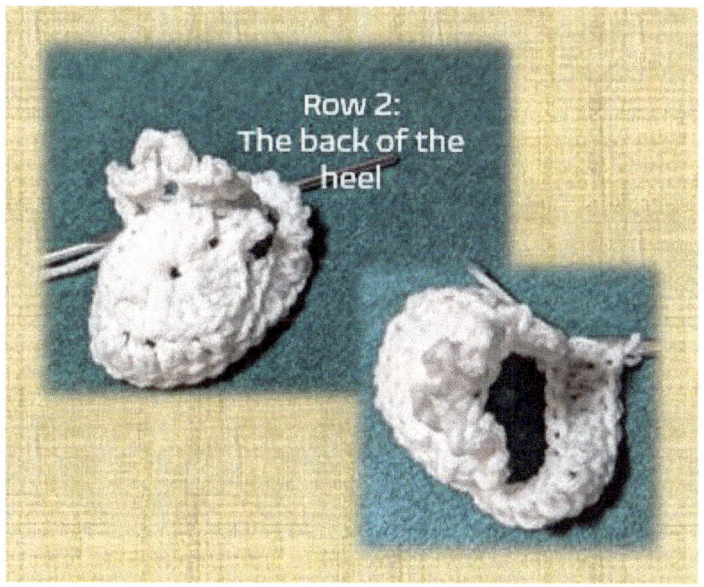

Row 3

- SC, Decrease by one SC in two loops. (sc, decrease 2sc) Repeat to end of row.

Row 4

- Decrease by one SC in two loops to end of row. (dec2sc)

Row 5

- Decrease by one SC in three loops (dec3sc three times.) Tie off. Pull knot and yarn into the foot and weave and trim.

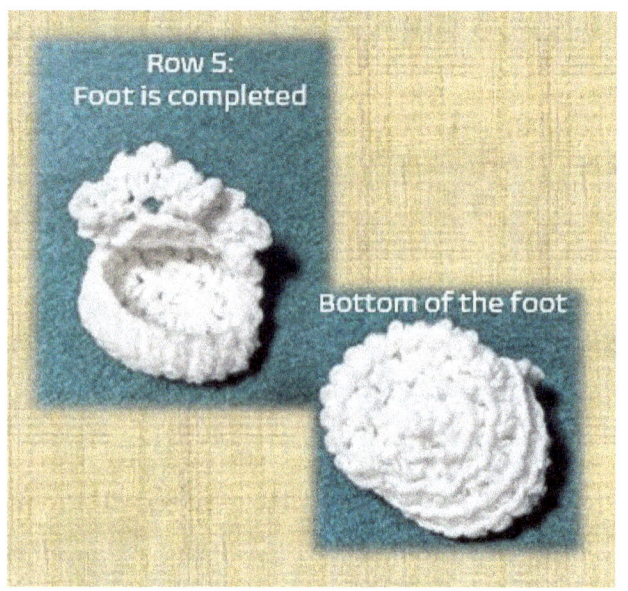

Cuff:

Row 1

- Attach with slip stitch directly behind first stitch of ruffle. [SC, Decrease by one SC in two loops]. Repeat [ ] until you get to other side of the ruffle. SC in the back (front to you now) loop of each ruffle. Slip stitch to close.

Row 2

- Chain 2 and turn. Begin working on the outside of bootie. DC in each stitch. Use the inside loops behind the ruffle to complete the ankle as a circle. Slip stitch to close.

Row 3
- Chain 2 and turn. DC in each stitch. Slip stitch to close.

Row 4
- Chain 2 and turn. DC behind each DC column of previous row. Last DC should be worked behind the turning chains of this and the previous row – you will have to fold down the cuff.
- Slip stitch to base of second row. Tie off and pull yarn inside bootie. Weave and trim

Row 4 of cuff

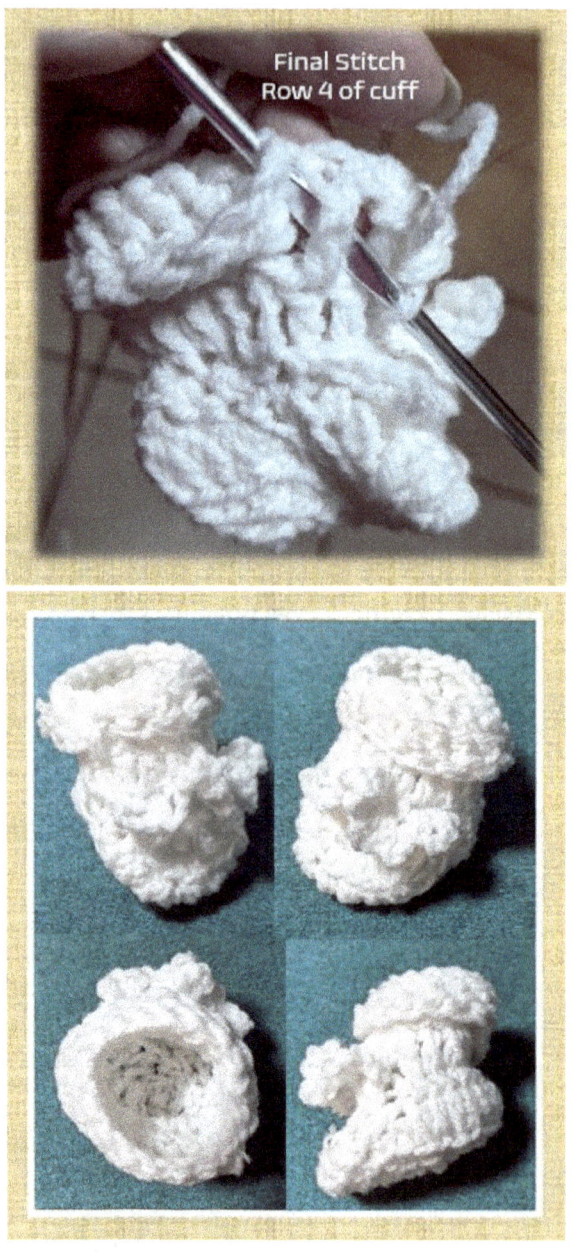

Make 2 for each pair . . .

ISAIAH 9:5

> For to us a child is born,
> a son will be given to us,
> and the government will be upon His shoulder.
> His Name will be called
> Wonderful Counselor,
> Mighty God
> My Father of Eternity,
> Prince of Peace.

I find it interesting that Jesus was fully man and fully God, and yet we lovingly remember Jesus as The Child. The Child which is a gift from God. We are often told that Jesus came as a reward for laboring for righteousness' sake, and obeying God's commandments and following His instructions. But no, The Child came as a gift, just as all children are gifts from God.

The pairing of adjective and noun in the second part of this verse is musical (and of course, now some of you have Handel's *Messiah* stuck in your head!) Not just someone who listens and gives advice, but a Wonderful Counselor. Not just a god (lower case g is intentional) but a Mighty God. A Father who will be our father forever. Not a conquering prince who slays all in his path, but a Prince of Peace.

As a parent, what kind of counselor are you? Are you a creator who makes all things good? Are you always living the role of parent? Do you govern your house with threats and a violent fist or with kindness and gentle guidance?

BASIC RIPPLE AFGHAN

One of the first things I ever identified as crocheted was a ripple afghan my father's mother gave us when I was four. It was all sorts of autumnal colors, and its pattern fascinated me. The ripple pattern can be adapted in so many ways: the length of the rises and falls, the stitch itself – or combinations of stitches, the thickness and the colors of the yarn, the size of the hook. Over the years, you can make each ripple afghan different with no two the same. There is no elaborate pattern one must follow, so it is the perfect project to sit in church or in front of the TV or in a waiting room and do.

Simple, yes, but there are secrets which must be adhered to in order to come out with a straight-edged, rectangular afghan.

A ripple consists of one rise and one fall. We'll call each rise and each fall **B** because they are the same length.

Each afghan has a certain number of the rise/fall **pairs**. We'll call those pairs **C**. For most afghans, 6 works well as C.

To gage the correct number of stitches to chain at the first, you multiply **2B with C** which we will call **A**.

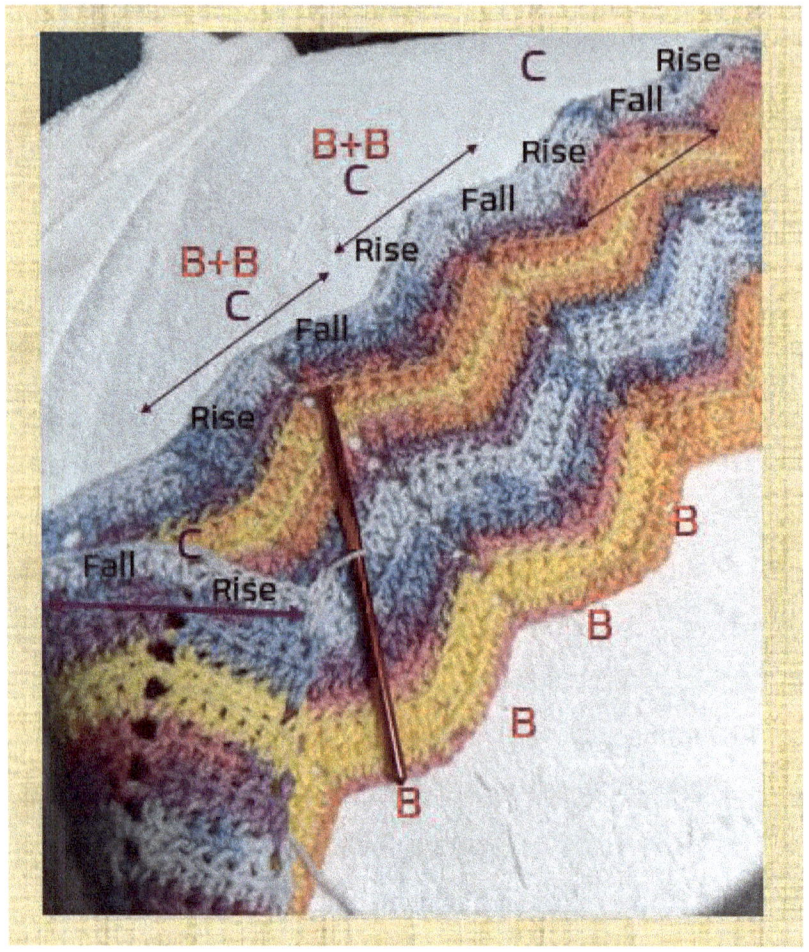

Infant ripples are made using size F hooks with a thickness of 3. Child ripples are size J hook with a thickness of 4. Both infant and child ripples are 7 stitches in the rise and 7 in the fall. Adult ripples are made using size J and thickness of 4 but have 9 stitches in the rise and 9 in the fall.

So infant/child ripples are 2 times 7 times 6 = 84 = A

Adult ripples are 2 times 9 times 6 = 108 = A

The beginning chain for any ripple is (2 times B times C) plus 1 or **A plus 1**. Infant/child = 85, adult = 109.

In all the rows, you skip 2 stitches at the valley.

For all rows, the mountain has (stitch, chain 2, stitch) in the previous chain space. The first stitch counts as the last stitch of rising B. The chain 2 is where each mountain top will be put. The next stitch counts as the first stitch of the falling B. So, the basic pattern looks like this: **(B-1), (stitch, chain 2, stitch), (B-1), skip 2 stitches.**

Examples: infant afghan is 6, (stitch, chain 2, stitch), 6, skip 2. Adult is 8, (stitch, chain 2, stitch), 8, skip 2.

Now, the secret to this project lies in how you do the first rise and the last fall of each row.

SECRET 1: THE FIRST RISE

For the second and following rows, you will chain 2 or 3 (depending on your stitch – 2 for sc or hdc; 3 for dc or tc), turn, and **skip the next stitch**, then crochet B-2 and then the last stitch of B in the chain space:

Chain 2or 3, skip one, (5 or 7) stitches, (stitch, chain 2, stitch to begin the next fall).

SECRET 2: THE LAST FALL

Crochet the (stitch which is the last of the previous rise, chain 2, stitch to begin the last fall) in the mountain top. Then crochet B-2 stitches. You will place the last stitch between the columns of the last and second to last stitches of the previous row. Not through the loops; through the columns:

(Stitch which is the last of the previous rise, chain 2, stitch to begin the last fall), (5 or 7) stitches, one stitch between the last columns. Chain 2 or 3, turn.

It is through these first and last stitches that you will crochet your border.

Borders are done along the top with a picot or clones kno or other fancy stitch at the peak and still skips the two stitches in the valley. Borders along the side are worked through the posts and then can be embellished with triangles or shells or just left as a bold, thick, plain HDC border.

2nd row of Side border with Clones knots

Rise & Fall of border with a picot at each apex

RIPPLE AFGHAN PATTERN

Chain A plus 1

Row 1:

- First rise and fall: skip 2 chains and begin first stitch in the third from the hook. A-1 stitches. Chain 2, 1 stitch in the same chain. A-1 stitches. Skip 2 stitches.
- Second rise and fall: A stitches. Chain 2, 1 stitch in the same chain. A-1 stitches. Skip 2 stitches.
- Third rise and fall: A stitches. Chain 2, 1 stitch in the same chain. A-1 stitches. Skip 2 stitches.
- Fourth rise and fall: A stitches. Chain 2, 1 stitch in the same chain. A-1 stitches. Skip 2 stitches.
- Fifth rise and fall: A stitches. Chain 2, 1 stitch in the same chain. A-1 stitches. Skip 2 stitches.
- Sixth (last) rise and fall: A stitches. Chain 2, 1 stitch in the same chain. A-2 stitches. Gather all remaining chain loops onto your hooks (if you've done it right, there should only be one) and crochet one stitch through them. Chain 2 or 3. Turn.

Row 2:
- First rise and fall: skip 2 stitches and begin first stitch in the third. A-2 stitches. In the chain space from the previous row, 1 stitch, chain 2, 1 stitch in the same chain space. A-1 stitches. Skip 2 stitches.
- Second rise and fall: A-1 stitches. In the chain space from the previous row, 1 stitch, chain 2, 1 stitch in the same chain space. A-1 stitches. Skip 2 stitches.
- Third, fourth, fifth rises and falls: Repeat second rise and fall
- Sixth (last) rise and fall: A-1 stitches. In the chain space from the previous row, 1 stitch, chain 2, 1 stitch in the same chain space. A-2 stitches. Skip 1 stitch. Place last stitch between the columns of the previous row. Chain 2 or 3. Turn.

Rows 3- however many you want to make it the length you desire: Repeat row 2.

Borders:

Frame your project by using hdc stitches for the first row of the border: Down the sides, place 2 hdc stitches in each column if the stitches were hdc, 3 if dc, 4 if tc.

Across the top, place one hdc stitch in each of the previous row's stitches, (stitch, chain 2, stitch) in the chain spaces, skip 2 in each valley.

Put three in each of the four corners.

Second row of the border: Down the sides: (sc, hdc, dc, tc, picot, tc, dc, hdc, sc) as a repeat – one in each stitch – through both loops. Across the top, place one stitch in each of the previous row's stitches. (hdc, picot, hdc) in the chain space of the peak of the row below. Skip 2 in each valley. Put three in each of the four corners. Slip stitch to close. Finish off. Weave in.

Note: picot is chain 3, sc stitch in third from hook. Advanced crocheters may use Clones Knot instead of a picot (see the instructions under Huggable Toys).

2 CHRONICLES 20:13, 31:18

All Judah was standing before *ADONAI*
with their infants, their wives and their children.
(20:13)

The genealogical registry included
all their little ones, their wives and sons and daughters
of the entire assembly.
Thus in their faithfulness they consecrated themselves
as holy.
(31:18)

Do your social media accounts include your children and grandchildren? Is your spouse listed? Could one read your social media account and know that you are consecrated faithfully to God's holiness?

Does your membership into a church or synagogue or temple include your children and your spouse? Are you known as a faithful follower and holy leader?

When you are counted by God, your accounting will include the gifts God gave you – your children and your spouse.

MINISTERING TO CHILDREN AND PARENTS WITH SPECIAL NEEDS

By Mark Koebernik

Ministering to a child with special needs and their family is both simple and complex at the same time. Simple in that all one needs to remember is to "Keep it Simple." It is also complex because it depends on either the mental and/or physical challenge of the child and maybe even their age.

There are many types of physical and mental challenges from Specific Learning Disabled (SLD), Vision Impaired (VI), hearing impaired (HI), behavioral and emotional disorders, among many others. There are also children with autism. This means you need to keep it simple. To keep it simple, don't use a lot of flowering, technical words. As much as I love reading the King James Version, it has many words that children do not understand. So, pick a Bible version that uses easy to understand words. It might be a good idea to use pictures when teaching children about the Bible because, like adults, children learn in different ways. Some are auditory learners, some are visual learners, and some students are kinesthetic learners; that is, they are hands-on learners. For these students, you might want to have the class draw or paint pictures of the story you are teaching them. However, you will also want to be careful of the amount of pictures you use as some children, especially those with autism, might be overly stimulated. So, keep pictures/drawings to a minimum.

There might be children who have trouble keeping still. For these students, create a play of the story you are teaching them and when possible or appropriate, have the students write the play. It is important to involve the students as much as possible. If they take ownership of the lesson, they might understand it better and longer.

In conclusion, not only does it matter what is said but how it is said or presented. Use a variety of teaching methods. Don't just sit/stand up in front of the class talking but involve the students! If possible, create a play of the story. In other words, consider using a variety of teaching methods in one lesson. The attention span of many students will probably be short, so you might consider breaking the lesson up into short pieces. You might want to talk about the story for a few minutes, then have the students draw pictures of the lesson, or have a whole group discussion about that particular part of the lesson. There are many ways one can use various teaching methods to minster to children and their families. You can use one method for the entire lesson or you can use multiple methods in one lesson. It will help you very much to know your audience.

About Mark Koebernik

Mark has a Master's Degree in Education from Florida Southern College. He has been in education since the late 1990's, including 5 years as a substitute teacher. For the last sixteen years, Mark has taught at all levels from elementary through college. Most of those years were in the field of special education. In addition to being a traditional classroom teacher, Mark has been an inclusion teacher, a resource teacher, and a self-contained teacher. He is certified to teach in both Louisiana and Florida.

JOSHUA 14:9

So Moses swore on that day saying:
'Surely the land on which your foot has trodden will be an inheritance to you and to your children forever, because you have fully followed *ADONAI* my God.'

Where do you walk? What places do you go to and meander or pace through? Is it a place you would like to inherit?

If not, perhaps you are walking in the wrong path and you should find a different place to travel.

Remember, your children also walk where you walk and will inherit what you inherit. Some things are genetically inherited, like addictive personalities and perfect pitch. Some things are behaviorally inherited, like abusive behaviors. But caring, honesty, kindness, love, joy, and belonging are also inherited.

What did you inherit from your parents? What will your children inherit from you?

BREAST-FEEDING MODESTY SHAWL

Beginner Pattern

STITCHES USED

Chain – With one loop on your hook, yarn-over, pull the yarn through the loop. You now have one (new) loop on the hook.

Double Crochet – DC - With one loop on your hook, yarn-over and put your hook through the loop in the row below. You now have 3 loops on the hook. Yarn-over and pull through one loop. You again have 3 loops on your hook. Yarn over and pull through 2 loops. You now have 2 loops on your hook. Yarn over

Slip Stitch – SS - With one loop on your hook, put your hook through the loop in the row below. You now have two loops on the hook. Yarn over and pull through both loops. You now have one (new) loop on the hook.

Fasten off - cut your yarn about 3 inches from your hook. Yarn-over and pull through the loop you have. Tug gently.

CONSTRUCTION

The shawl is made from the top center expanding out equally to each side and down the center with each row. The loaves consist of sets of 2 DC. The fish consists of 5-chains with SS attaching them to the center of the previous row's 1 chain spots for the first row, and then the center of the previous row's 5 chain space. There are 5 rows of loaves, then 5 rows of fish, and this repeats until the shawl is the length and width desired. The final border is a row of half-double crochet stitches along the top, 2 per sideways DC, and then a ruffle, shell, or picot or Clones knot along the sides. The center always remains [2 dc, chain 2, 2 dc] in the 2-chain space. The first and last sets are always [2 dc, chain 1, 3 DC] (last) and [chain 3, 2 DC, chain 1, 2 DC] (first).

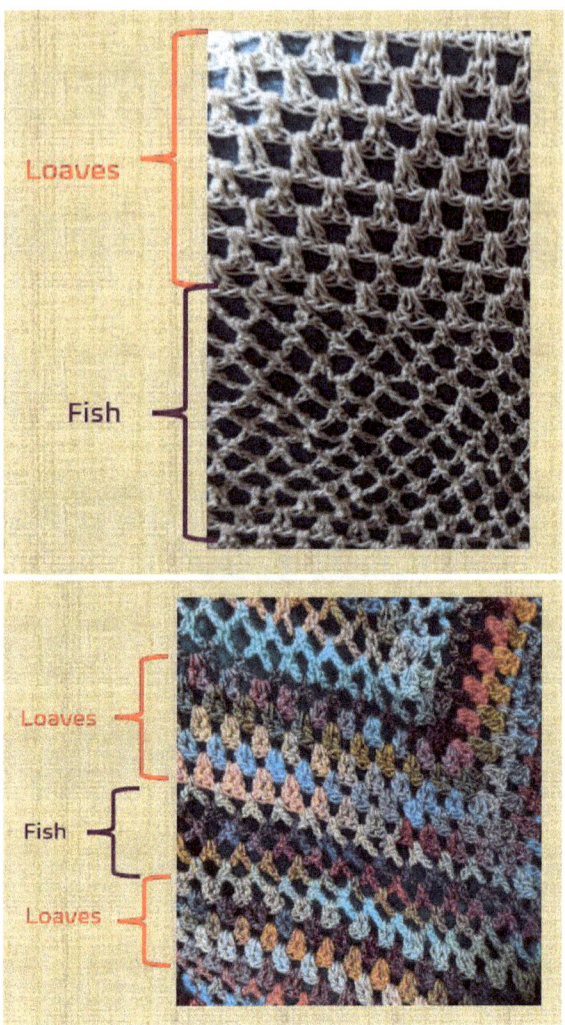

PATTERN

BEGINNING CIRCLE

Chain 3. Insert hook into the loop of the first chain (the one farthest from your hook; the one right next to your knot.) SS (Yarn over and pull through both loops.) Chain 3 (counts as 1 DC now and throughout). Turn.

Row 1 (Loaves)
Into the center of the circle you just made, put 1 dc, chain 2, 2 dc (center set made).
Chain 3, turn.

Row 2 (Loaves)
In base of 3-chain (which counts as a DC here and throughout), put 2 more DC. Chain 1.
In the 2-chain space of the center set, [2 DC, chain 2, 2 DC].
Chain 1.
3 DC between the 2nd and 3rd dc of previous row.
Chain 3, turn.

Row 3 (Loaves)
In base of 3-chain (which counts as a DC here and throughout), put 2 more DC. Chain 1.
Put 2 DC in the chain-1 space of previous row, chain 1.
In the 2-chain space of the center set, [2 DC, chain 2, 2 DC].
Chain 1.
Put 2 DC in the chain-1 space of previous row, chain 1.
3 DC between the 2nd and 3rd dc of previous row.
Chain 3, turn.

Row 4 (Loaves)
In base of 3-chain (which counts as a DC here and throughout), put 2 more DC. Chain 1.
[Put 2 DC in the chain-1 space of previous row, chain 1.] twice
In the 2-chain space of the center set, [2 DC, chain 2, 2 DC].
Chain 1.
[Put 2 DC in the chain-1 space of previous row, chain

1.] twice
3 DC between the 2nd and 3rd dc of previous row.
Chain 3, turn.

Row 5 (Loaves)
In base of 3-chain (which counts as a DC here and throughout), put 2 more DC. Chain 1.
[Put 2 DC in the chain-1 space of previous row, chain 1.] three times
In the 2-chain space of the center set, [2 DC, chain 2, 2 DC].
Chain 1.
[Put 2 DC in the chain-1 space of previous row, chain 1.] three times
3 DC between the 2nd and 3rd dc of previous row.
Chain 3, turn.

Row 6 (Fish)

In base of 3-chain (which counts as a DC here and throughout), put 2 more DC. Chain 1.

Put 2 DC in the chain-1 space of previous row, chain 3.

[SS in chain-1 space of previous row. Chain 5.] twice

SS in chain-1 space of previous row. Chain 3.

In the 2-chain space of the center set, [2 DC, chain 2, 2 DC]. Chain 3.

[SS in chain-1 space of previous row. Chain 5.] twice

SS in chain-1 space of previous row. Chain 3.

Put 2 DC in the next chain-1 space of previous row, chain 1.

3 DC between the 2nd and 3rd dc of previous row. Chain 3, turn.

CARING FOR CHILDREN THROUGH CROCHET

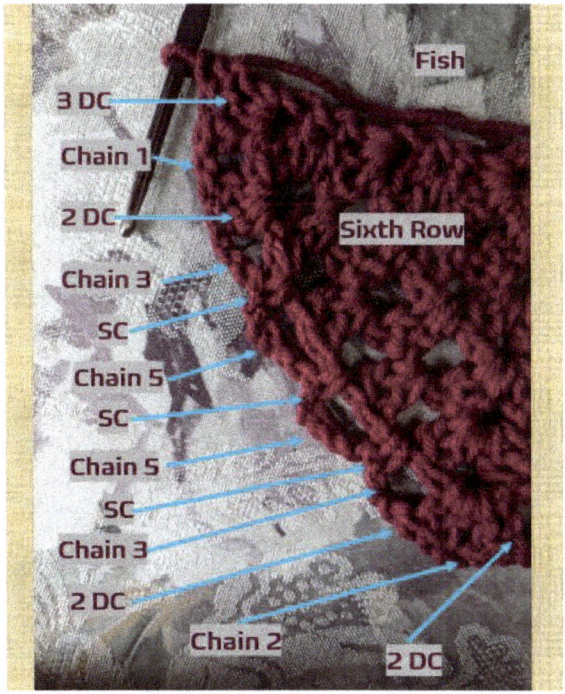

Row 7 (Fish)

In base of 3-chain (which counts as a DC here and throughout), put 2 more DC. Chain 1.

Put 2 DC in the chain-1 space of previous row, chain 3.

[SS in chain-5 space of previous row. Chain 5.] three times

SS in chain-3 space of previous row. Chain 3.

In the 2-chain space of the center set, [2 DC, chain 2, 2 DC]. Chain 3.

[SS in chain-3 space of previous row. Chain 5.] three times

SS in chain-5 space of previous row. Chain 3.

Put 2 DC in the next chain-1 space of previous row, chain 1.

3 DC between the 2nd and 3rd dc of previous row. Chain 3, turn.

Seventh Row

Fish

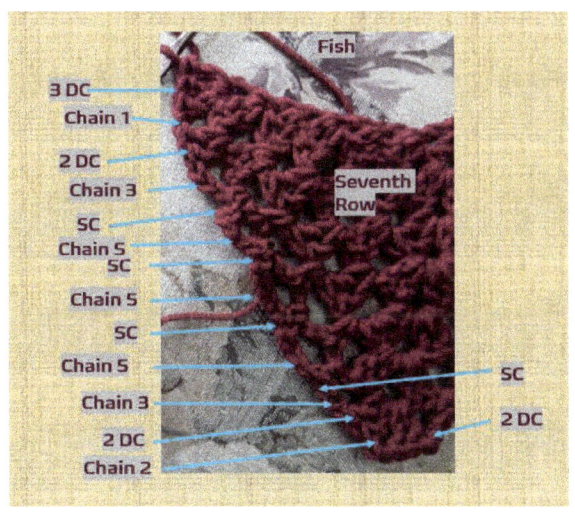

Row 8 (Fish)

In base of 3-chain (which counts as a DC here and throughout), put 2 more DC. Chain 1.

Put 2 DC in the chain-3 space of previous row, chain 3.

[SS in chain-5 space of previous row. Chain 5.] four times

SS in chain-3 space of previous row. Chain 3.

In the 2-chain space of the center set, [2 DC, chain 2, 2 DC]. Chain 3.

[SS in chain-3 space of previous row. Chain 5.] four times

SS in chain-3 space of previous row. Chain 3.

Put 2 DC in the next chain-1 space of previous row, chain 1.

3 DC between the 2nd and 3rd dc of previous row. Chain 3, turn.

Row 9 (Fish)
In base of 3-chain (which counts as a DC here and throughout), put 2 more DC. Chain 1.
Put 2 DC in the chain-1 space of previous row, chain 3.
[SS in chain-3 space of previous row. Chain 5.] five times
SS in chain-3 space of previous row. Chain 3.
In the 2-chain space of the center set, [2 DC, chain 2, 2 DC]. Chain 3.
[SS in chain-3 space of previous row. Chain 5.] five times
SS in chain-3 space of previous row. Chain 3.
Put 2 DC in the next chain-1 space of previous row, chain 1.
3 DC between the 2nd and 3rd dc of previous row. Chain 3, turn.

Row 10 (Fish)
In base of 3-chain (which counts as a DC here and throughout), put 2 more DC. Chain 1.
Put 2 DC in the chain-1 space of previous row, chain 3.
[SS in chain-3 space of previous row. Chain 5.] six times
SS in chain-3 space of previous row. Chain 3.
In the 2-chain space of the center set, [2 DC, chain 2, 2 DC]. Chain 3.
[SS in chain-3 space of previous row. Chain 5.] six times
SS in chain-3 space of previous row. Chain 3.
Put 2 DC in the next chain-1 space of previous row, chain 1.
3 DC between the 2nd and 3rd dc of previous row. Chain 3, turn.

Row 11 (Loaves)
In base of 3-chain (which counts as a DC here and throughout), put 2 more DC. Chain 1.
Put 2 DC in the chain-3 space of previous row, chain 1.
[Put 2 DC in the next chain-5 space of previous row, chain 1.] six times
Put 2 DC in the chain-3 space of previous row, chain 1.
In the 2-chain space of the center set, [2 DC, chain 2, 2 DC].
Chain 1.
Put 2 DC in the chain-3 space of previous row, chain 1.
[Put 2 DC in the next chain-5 space of previous row, chain 1.] six times
Put 2 DC in the chain-3 space of previous row, chain 1.
3 DC between the 2nd and 3rd dc of previous row.
Chain 3, turn.

Row 12 (Loaves)
In base of 3-chain (which counts as a DC here and throughout), put 2 more DC. Chain 1.
[Put 2 DC in the chain space of previous row, chain 1.] ten times
In the 2-chain space of the center set, [2 DC, chain 2, 2 DC].
Chain 1.
[Put 2 DC in the chain space of previous row, chain 1.] Ten times
3 DC between the 2nd and 3rd dc of previous row.
Chain 3, turn.

Row 13 (Loaves)
In base of 3-chain (which counts as a DC here and throughout), put 2 more DC. Chain 1.
[Put 2 DC in the chain space of previous row, chain 1.] eleven times
In the 2-chain space of the center set, [2 DC, chain 2, 2 DC].
Chain 1.
[Put 2 DC in the chain space of previous row, chain 1.] eleven times
3 DC between the 2nd and 3rd dc of previous row.
Chain 3, turn.

Row 14 (Loaves)
In base of 3-chain (which counts as a DC here and throughout), put 2 more DC. Chain 1.
[Put 2 DC in the chain space of previous row, chain 1.] twelve times
In the 2-chain space of the center set, [2 DC, chain 2, 2 DC].
Chain 1.
[Put 2 DC in the chain space of previous row, chain 1.] twelve times
3 DC between the 2nd and 3rd dc of previous row.
Chain 3, turn.

Row 15 (Loaves)
In base of 3-chain (which counts as a DC here and throughout), put 2 more DC. Chain 1.
[Put 2 DC in the chain space of previous row, chain 1.] thirteen times

In the 2-chain space of the center set, [2 DC, chain 2, 2 DC].
Chain 1.
[Put 2 DC in the chain space of previous row, chain 1.] thirteen times
3 DC between the 2nd and 3rd dc of previous row.
Chain 3, turn.

Row 16 (Fish)
In base of 3-chain (which counts as a DC here and throughout), put 2 more DC. Chain 1.
Put 2 DC in the chain-1 space of previous row, chain 3.
[SS in chain space of previous row. Chain 5.] twelve times
SS in chain-3 space of previous row. Chain 3.
In the 2-chain space of the center set, [2 DC, chain 2, 2 DC]. Chain 3.
[SS in chain space of previous row. Chain 5.] twelve times
SS in chain-3 space of previous row. Chain 3.
Put 2 DC in the next chain-1 space of previous row, chain 1.
3 DC between the 2nd and 3rd dc of previous row.
Chain 3, turn.

Row 17 (Fish)
In base of 3-chain (which counts as a DC here and throughout), put 2 more DC. Chain 1.
Put 2 DC in the chain-1 space of previous row, chain 3.
SS in chain-3 space of previous row. Chain 5.
[SS in chain space of previous row. Chain 5.] thirteen

times
SS in chain-3 space of previous row. Chain 3.
In the 2-chain space of the center set, [2 DC, chain 2, 2 DC]. Chain 3.
SS in chain-3 space of previous row. Chain 5.
[SS in chain space of previous row. Chain 5.] thirteen times
SS in chain-3 space of previous row. Chain 3.
Put 2 DC in the next chain-1 space of previous row, chain 1.
3 DC between the 2nd and 3rd dc of previous row. Chain 3, turn.

Row 18 (Fish)
In base of 3-chain (which counts as a DC here and throughout), put 2 more DC. Chain 1.
Put 2 DC in the chain-1 space of previous row, chain 3.
SS in chain-3 space of previous row. Chain 5.
[SS in chain space of previous row. Chain 5.] fourteen times
SS in chain-3 space of previous row. Chain 3.
In the 2-chain space of the center set, [2 DC, chain 2, 2 DC]. Chain 3.
SS in chain-3 space of previous row. Chain 5.
[SS in chain space of previous row. Chain 5.] fourteen times
SS in chain-3 space of previous row. Chain 3.
Put 2 DC in the next chain-1 space of previous row, chain 1.
3 DC between the 2nd and 3rd dc of previous row. Chain 3, turn.

Row 19 (Fish)
In base of 3-chain (which counts as a DC here and throughout), put 2 more DC. Chain 1.
Put 2 DC in the chain-1 space of previous row, chain 3.
[SS in chain space of previous row. Chain 5.] fifteen times
SS in chain-3 space of previous row. Chain 3.
In the 2-chain space of the center set, [2 DC, chain 2, 2 DC]. Chain 3.
[SS in chain space of previous row. Chain 5.] fifteen times
SS in chain-3 space of previous row. Chain 3.
Put 2 DC in the next chain-1 space of previous row, chain 1.
3 DC between the 2nd and 3rd dc of previous row. Chain 3, turn.

Row 20 (Fish)
In base of 3-chain (which counts as a DC here and throughout), put 2 more DC. Chain 1.
Put 2 DC in the chain-1 space of previous row, chain 3.
SS in chain-3 space of previous row. Chain 5.
[SS in chain space of previous row. Chain 5.] sixteen times
SS in chain-3 space of previous row. Chain 3.
In the 2-chain space of the center set, [2 DC, chain 2, 2 DC]. Chain 3.
SS in chain-3 space of previous row. Chain 5.
[SS in chain space of previous row. Chain 5.] sixteen times

SS in chain-3 space of previous row. Chain 3.
Put 2 DC in the next chain-1 space of previous row, chain 1.
3 DC between the 2nd and 3rd dc of previous row.
Chain 3, turn.

Continue 5 rows of loaves followed by 5 rows of fish until the shawl is finger-tip to finger-tip or longer.
Finish with 5 rows of loaves.

Border:
After the final Chain 3, pivot so that you are now working along the sides of the DC (across the top, through the original center, and down to the other tip).
Work 2 HDC in each side of the DCs.
Chain 3.
Pivot so that you are again working in the top of the last row worked.
In base of 3-chain (which counts as a DC here and throughout), put 2 more DC. Chain 1.
Work [6 DC, chain 1] in the chain spaces along this row to the center set.
In the 2-chain space of the center set, [9 DC]. Chain 1.
Work [6 DC, chain 1] in the chain spaces along this row to the final set.
3 DC between the 2nd and 3rd dc of previous row.
SS into the chain-3 of the border. Finish off. Weave tail into the hdc stitches of the border.

CARING FOR CHILDREN THROUGH CROCHET

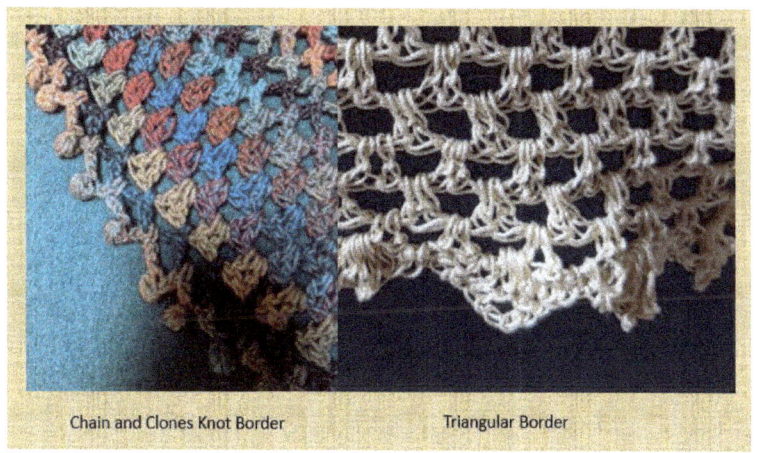

Chain and Clones Knot Border | Triangular Border

DEUTERONOMY 31:12

Gather the people—
the men and women and little ones,
and the outsider within your town gates—
so they may hear and so they may learn,
and they will fear ADONAI your God and take care to do
all the words of this Torah.

Children watch and repeat what you do. They mimic your actions and echo your beliefs. When they are in your car, you demonstrate all the safety skills that they will learn. When you speak to a waitress or a stranger, you are teaching them how to treat people. Have you taught your children to disrespect private property by tossing trash out the car window? Have you encouraged your children to disregard city ordinances and laws by ignoring the parking signs or traffic lights? If so, when they wind up in jail, prison, or the cemetery, I hope you realize they were simply following your example.

BUTTON COVERS

Button covers are cute and can make shirts fun. You can also put the designs on small drawer pulls or fan pulls. You can make them into banners by crocheting them together in chains. They can serve as very memorable gift tags. By adding a foundation ring, you can use them as the center of granny squares. These are based on the same skills you have already learned and can be made from left-over balls of yarn.

Make 6 or a dozen of each. Stick with traditional colors or use variegated or bizarre colors. Have fun!

Bears

Begin by chaining 6. Slip stitch to join into a circle. Chain 2. 11 HDC in the circle, weaving in the tail as you go. Slip Stitch to the chain.

Row 1

Chain 2 (counts as a DC). DC in the base of the chain, then 2 DC through both loops of each stitch around the circle. Slip stitch to the chain. Chain 1.

Row 2

SC in next 4 stitches. In both loops of the next stitch, put 8 DC (makes one ear). SC around the circle for the next 16 stiches. Through both loops of the next stitch (the last of this row), put 8 DC (makes second ear). Slip stitch to the chain. Fasten off. Weave in.

Embroider simple eyes. Tie a ribbon as the bow tie for the male bear or between the ears for a female bear.

Hearts

Begin by chaining 6. Slip stitch to join into a circle.

Row 1

Chain 2. 17 HDC in the circle.
Slip Stitch to the chain. Chain 1.

Row 2

Crochet one set in each stitch:
SC, 2 HDC, 2 DC, 2 TC, 2 DC, 2 HDC, SC, SC, (SC, CHAIN 2, SC, in the same stitch = point of the heart), SC, SC, 2 HDC, 2 DC, 2 TC, 2 DC, 2 HDC, SC, slip stitch into first chain.

Row 3

Crochet one set in each stitch:
SC, 2 HDC, 2 DC, 2 TC, 2 DC, 2 HDC, SC in the next 7

stitches, (SC, chain-2, SC in the chain space from row 2), SC in next 7 stitches, 2 HDC, 2 DC, 2 TC, 2 DC, 2 HDC, slip stitch into first stitch. Fasten off and weave in. Pluck it into shape.

Roses

Leaves:

Chain 6, slips stitch into a circle, chain 1.

Row 1
10 HDC into the circle, slip stitch to first stitch, chain 1

Row 2
[In the front loops of first stitch: SC. HDC, 3 DC, HDC, SC Slip stitch through both loops of next stitch, chain 1.] Repeat 4 more times until you have 5 petals.
(You may tie off and weave in here to make single layer roses).

Row 3 (work in the back side of the flower)
Chain 3 and slip stitch into the space between the petals.] Repeat 4 more times until you have a foundation ring with 5 chains.

Row 4 (Work with the flower facing you. Fold down each petal to crochet in the foundation chain behind it.)
[SC, HDC, DC, 3 TC, DC, HDC, SC. Slip stitch in the post between the foundation chains.] Repeat 4 more times until you have 5 petals.
(You may tie off and weave in here to make double-layer roses).

Row 5 (work in the back side of the flower)
Chain 2 to reach the back loop of the first row's first petal. Slip stitch into that back loop. [Chain 3, slip stitch into the next petal's back loop.] Repeat until you have 5 foundation ring chains.

Row 6 (Turn to work with the flower facing you. Fold down the petals to work in the chain spaces.)
In each chain space: SC, HDC, 2DC, 3TC, 2DC, HDC, SC. Slip stitch in the post between the foundation chains.] Repeat 4 more times until you have 5 petals. (If you are going to use this as the center of a granny square, add leaves, sew it onto a barrette, or applique it onto something, make one more foundational ring of 5 3-chains.)
Finish off and weave in.

DEUTERONOMY 28:4

Blessed will be the fruit of your womb,
the produce of your soil,
and the offspring of your livestock—
the increase of your herds and the young of your flock.

I have a plastic dinner tray that depicts a lovely farm scene. There are sheep and a milk cow and her calf, puppies and a kitten or two, chickens with chicks, and a field full of vegetables. I can't help but hope that my mansion in heaven will be very similar to this scene.

Abundance. That is such a wonderful and hopeful word. The Law of Abundance is that there is an abundance in all things. There is no want that cannot be filled, no hunger that cannot be satisfied, no sorrow that cannot be comforted.

How wonderful the world would be if your children and all that you achieve would be blessed. God promises it will be so. Perhaps it isn't true now, but one day it will be.

PARENTING AS A MINISTRY

By Tif E. Boots

I will be the first to admit I am far from the perfect parent. I get frustrated, I lose my temper. I believe children should have chores and be expected to complete them. Chores teach responsibility and help with time management. I expect those chores to be done right to the best of their ability and to be done in a timely manner to encourage time management. As a parent, it is not my job to be a friend, it is my duty to prepare my child for life and for the world around them. As children, I am sure they think I am a mean mom. I know I irritate them, and they think I am too strict. They look at friends who have phones and unlimited access to the internet and social media. Friends that do not have chores or a limit on screen time. I am sure from my child's point of view that I am unreasonable, and I just do not understand. When they are adults, I hope they look back and understand the methods to my madness.

As a child myself I did not exactly have chores, but my family had their own business. My brother and I were expected to work the counters, prepare, and serve food, set up and tear down the equipment. We learned how to manage time, count back change, load, unload and repack the stock truck. As a child I would look at my friends who were able to participate in summer sports and camps. Those who were part of the boy or girl scouts. They went camping with their families while I was stuck working long hours around heat lamps and hot fryers in the dead of summer. I thought I hated it. Looking back, I know if I had not been raised that way, I would not be the person I am today. I feel that my childhood gave me a firm footing in life. I was taught at a young age how to be responsible, how to work, how to survive and how to get along with people from all walks of life.

A definition of minister is to attend to the needs of someone. I am not a religious person. I believe in my lord and savior. I, however, am not comfortable preaching. I will not deny my lord, but I am much better at ministering to the needs of someone. I know I am not perfect; I am a simple sinner. The best I can do is apologize when I've been wrong and learn from my mistakes. As a parent I try to minister to all the needs of my children. I know I am not perfect; they have all they need to live, I show understanding and empathy for the things they see as problems. They know they can come to me when mistakes are made. I am not afraid to apologize to my children when I have been wrong or overwhelmed and lost my temper. I believe that trying to be a good person, admitting my faults, will help to guide my children into being the people they are meant to be. From watching me, I hope they learn it's okay to mess up and everyone is deserving of love and respect. From the expectations I set for both them and myself I hope they learn the value of hard work, friendship and family.

Sometimes the best way to minister to a child is to listen without judgement, do not be afraid to admit when you're wrong and apologize when needed. Children deserve respect as much as everyone else. They see when you are humble enough to admit your own mistakes and shortcomings. They will learn and develop into the people they are meant to be by the examples you set every day.

About Tif E. Boots

Tiffany is the author of the wonderful series of children's books – **Brutus and Friends**.

She made front page news when she was born alongside Route 7 in Ohio! After her parents separated and her mom remarried, she was moved to Arizona. In the early years of her high school, Tif's parents separated, and she found herself alone. She did not let that stop her as she moved into a travel trailer parked at a friend's house and worked two jobs while completing high school. She graduated in 2000.

Tiffany began her working life when she was six years old as a bus girl in her family's concession stand business at local fairs in Arizona and Michigan. She soon was able to operate and manage her own food stand. Tiffany has had a wide variety of work experiences over the years. She began as a carny, worked fast food, photo technician, corrections officer, hospital kitchen employee, and a juvenile mental health aide for a residential behavior unit. She then fell into a career as a Certified Nurse's Aide and found her passion working with hospice patients.

Tiffany was married and had her first daughter in 2004. She then separated from her husband. Eventually she found her way back to her high school sweetheart and was blessed with a second daughter. Tiffany and her family moved again and have settled in Lakeland, Florida.

In her spare time, Tiffany enjoys painting and spending time on the water or at amusement parks with her family. Although her life has had its ups and downs, and her share of hardships, Tiffany is always working to make other people's lives as easy as possible.

DEUTERONOMY 4:40

You must keep His statutes and His *mitzvot*, which I am commanding you today, so that it may go well with you and with your children after you, and so that you may prolong your days in the land that *Adonai* your God is giving you for all time.

So, what happens when things don't go well? When your children have problems or get into trouble or don't live up to your expectations? Sometimes you feel that you are living on an alien planet. I remember a t-shirt that said, "This is not the life I ordered." The implication is that someone else is to blame. The child didn't practice his violin and never got to be first chair at the Met. The child just doesn't understand why your hobby is so exhilarating and finally refuses to join you. She gets pregnant. He gets on drugs. Their hair is too long or too short or they spend too much time on video games or on the phone.

Step back for a moment and identify who is at the center of this drama. Not the child; you are.

Now go back and reread Deuteronomy 4:40. Who should be at the center of things? God should. Once you place God at the center, things will "go well for you and for your children." Things will go well spiritually, and you will live in the place God wants you to be.

CROCHETED EGG RATTLES

Materials:

Plastic eggs

Non-toxic beads or beans (like lentil or black-eyed peas)

Size G crochet hook

Various colors (remnants) of 3-weight yarns

Hot-glue gun and sticks

Eggs:

Place 1 teaspoon of non-toxic beads or beans inside one plastic egg. Hot glue the rim. Press and seal. Set aside until cool.

Do this for as many eggs as you want.

Crochet:

Chain 3, slip stitch into a circle.

Row 1: Chain 2. 12 DC in circle, slip stitch to the chain-2 (13 stitches in all)

Row 2: Chain 2, put 1 DC into both loops of each stitch of the previous row, slip stitch into chain-2.

Row 3: Chain 2. [Put 1 sc in both loops of stitch, put 2 sc in both loops of next stitch.] Repeat [ ] around. Slip stitch to chain-2.

Rows 4, 5, and 6: Chain 2. In back loop: 1 HDC in each stitch around, Slip stitch to chain-2.

Turn crochet so it is right-side out.

Choose an egg which matches or blends well with the yarn. Place egg inside crochet, bottom-side down.

Row 7: Chain 1. In both loops, [Put 1 sc in both loops of stitch, decrease with 1 sc in both loops of next 2 stitches.] Repeat [ ] around. Slip stitch to chain-1. Gently shape the egg sack around the egg.

Eighth (Last) row: chain 1. Hook 3 more stitches through both loops. Yarn over and pull through 4 loops on hook. Hook 4 more stitches through both loops. Yarn over and pull through 5 loops on hook. Hook 2 more stitches through both loops. Yarn over and pull through 3 loops on hook. Chain 1. Finish off. Weave tail between crochet and egg.

To tie on yarn, crochet so the knot is under the fabric. Repeat for each egg.

CARING FOR CHILDREN THROUGH CROCHET

MATTHEW 2:11

And when they came into the house, they saw the child with his mother Miriam; and they fell down and worshiped him.
Then, opening their treasures, they presented to him gifts of gold, frankincense, and myrrh.

Gold symbolizes wealth, prosperity, love, and lasting relationships as well as passion, creativity, and transformation. [2]

Frankincense has been known to help with arthritis, digestion, and asthma.[3]

---

[2] Linda Callaway, "gold: symbolism, meanings, and history," Symbol Genie, October 8, 2022, https://symbolgenie.com/gold-symbolism-meanings.

[3] Alina Petre, MS, RD (NL) Medically reviewed by Jillian Kubala, MS, RD, Nutrition February 23, 2023 "5 Benefits and Uses of Frankincense — and 7 Myths," *Healthline*, https://www.healthline.com/nutrition/frankincense.

Myrrh is an antibiotic, and can kill parasites and mold, including *Aspergillus niger*, (aka black mold) and *A. flavus* which causes food to spoil.[4]

So Frankincense is used to improve inward, physical health. Myrrh is used to clean and disinfect. And Gold is used to improve spiritual health.

It's not what they gave the Child that is important; it is what those things represented.

What do you give to your children, and why?

---

[4] Marsha McCulloch, MS, RD "11 Surprising Benefits and Uses of Myrrh Oil." January 4, 2019, *Healthline*, https://www.healthline.com/nutrition/myrrh-oil.

FINGER PUPPETS

If you have been crocheting for a few dozen years, you will have accumulated a number of similar patterns, merged them into *tried and true* patterns and made some adaptations of your own. This is what I have done with my finger puppet patterns.

A finger puppet is basically a small tube with decorations. Finger puppets can be used to tell a story (with at least 4 characters) or make up a story (with at least 4 different characters). They can all be the same character, as long as the story is fun and the children enjoy them.

So here are basics on how to start your finger puppet, followed by several details for specific animals or facial hair or embroidery suggestions.

Basically, make the tube body and embellish it as your imagination leads you to do.

Materials

Hook -- sizes E, F, or G depending on the yarn. The point is to make the stitches tight so that nothing shows through.

Yarn – baby, fingering, or worsted. The point is to make the stitches tight so that nothing shows through.

Embroidery thread or scrap yarn for details

Glue-on eyes if the recipients are not going to put these puppets in their mouths.

Yarn needle.

Basic Body

Row 1: Chain 3, join as circle, chain 1. SC 6 inside the circle.

Row 2: 2 SC in each stitch.

Row 3: [2 SC in one stitch then 1 SC in the next.] Repeat around. (You may use a row marker, but you really don't need to since you are crocheting for length, not number of rows.)

Rows 4 – the length you desire (usually 12-15): SC around. Change colors or add details in the correct places desired while you crochet the body. For example, eyes should be put in on Row 6.

The last row should be HDC, then slip stitch the last one, fasten off and weave in the tail.

Details

Braids: On Row 3 on either side of the face. Take 2 pieces of yarn several inches in length. Fold in two and pull the center through a stitch (as you would fringe). Pull the yarn through the center loop. Then braid the yarn until it's almost used up. Tie with yarn or ribbon. Do this for both sides of the face.

Beard or hair bun: Chain 3, join in circle. 4SC in circle. Slip stitch to first stitch. Chain 2, 2 SC in each stitch. Slip stitch to first stitch. Chain 2. Dec2sc together around (4 stitches), slip stitch. Fasten off with 2 inch tail. Use the tail to attach the bun to the top of the head or the beard to the bottom of the mouth.

Whiskers: Pull the center of two pieces of yarn through the appropriate place and then pull the tails through the center, as one would do a fringe. Take the tails and separate the plies. Use a sharp edge of scissors to curl the untwisted yarn (like you would paper ribbons on a gift). You can also use embroidery thread in place of yarn.

Tight Fur or Scales: starting at the bottom of the puppet, SC on the top loops of the area desired, weaving across the path without ending. Second row, turn and do DC or TC in the top loops of the SC in the area, allowing them to overlap.

Furry Manes: You'll need a pencil. Starting at the bottom of the puppet, SC on the top loops of the area desired, weaving across the path without ending. Second row, turn and do DC or TC in the top loops of the SC and around the pencil in the area, allowing them to overlap.

Striped animals: The main color is used, with the secondary (stripe) color used for every third row: 3, 6, 9, 12, 15.

Normal Ears: Make 2. Chain 2, (sc, chain 3, sc) in second chain from hook. Finish off and sew ears to the head.

Bunny or Mule ears: Make 2. Chain 2, (dc, chain 3, dc) in second chain from hook. Finish off and sew ears to the head.

Tails, trunks, tusks, other thin appendages: Adjust length as desired. Chain 13, sc in second chain from hook and the next 11 chains. Finish off and sew to the specific area of the body.

Elephant Ears:

Right ear:

Row 1: chain 2, 4 sc in second chain from hook, chain 1, turn. (4 sc)
Row 2: 2 sc in first sc, 1 sc in each of the next 3 stitches, ch 1, turn. (5 sc)
Row 3: 2 sc in first sc, 1 sc in each of the next 4 stitches, finish off, weave in end. (6 sc)

Left ear:

Follow the pattern for the right ear until row 3.
Row 3: 1 sc in each of the next 4 sc, 2 sc in last sc, finish off, weave in ends. (6 sc)

CARING FOR CHILDREN THROUGH CROCHET

Finger Puppets

Octopus Finger Puppet

Alien Finger Puppet

Frog Finger Puppet

Buddy Finger Puppet

Add hair, a hat, clothes, anything to individualize this person puppet.

Queen Finger Puppet

Have fun making creative hair-styles.

MATTHEW 7:11; LUKE 11:13

If you then, being evil, know how to give good gifts to your children, how much more will your Father in heaven give good things to those who ask Him!
(Matthew)

¹³ If you then, being evil, know how to give good gifts to your children, how much more will your heavenly Father give the *Ruach ha-Kodesh* to those who ask Him!
(Luke)

I always dreaded the week after my students returned from Winter Break. These normally sweet and companionable children would suddenly turn into competitive divas, strutting in their new clothes and sneakers, or showing off their new electric device or jewelry or sports equipment. Those students who rarely had a pencil, crayons, or paper were usually the ones with the most expensive gifts, while those who were always depended on to loan an extra pencil, crayons, or paper, sat blinking and silent in the sudden and extravagant wealth of their peers. All students seem to know that this sudden and thin veneer of gifts would not last long and wouldn't be repeated again with any certainty. Good gifts – being dependable and generous – are far better than extravagant, usually meaningless gifts. Children realize this. Parents realize this. And God demonstrates this.

MINISTERING TO NEW PARENTS AND GRANDPARENTS

By Jerry Francis

I have been both a new parent and a new grandparent, so I know firsthand some of the challenges. Even if you have not had the experience, you may know someone who has. More than likely, the word hectic may come to mind. If you are a new grandparent, you want to put everything aside to help your children because you know what it means to be a new parent. There are obvious opportunities for you to help those in their new role, such as making them a meal or offering to take care of something. They must juggle their available time carefully, and something always has to give. From my own first-child experiences and as a grandparent, I must admit that spirituality is a part of life we feel we are sacrificing. I have also encountered situations where someone's faith is already hanging in the balance so it is even easier to put faith aside. However, I have learned that we should look at these situations from a different perspective.

Using myself as an example, as a grandparent, with two very young grandchildren, one of whom is not crawling yet. I want to help my daughter and son-in-law and be with my grandchildren as much as possible. My wife and I spend weekends at my daughter's and her husband's house, giving them a little breathing space. If you have been a parent or a new grandparent, you know the sacrifices include missed weekly church services. If you are used to prayer and being with believers, it sometimes feels like a tradeoff to spend time away from your faith community. Even with my pastoral ministry degree, I am sometimes uncertain about what to do. I realize how easy it is to miss an important part of who you are by even occasionally not attending church. However, there is an offset by considering how much joy that child, parent, or grandparent receives. If you are a grandparent, doesn't it also bring you joy to offer it? *I must remind myself that we are also called to go into the world with the gifts we have.* I know it will not be long before I am back with my faith community sharing the stories of wonder.

I have ideas about what we can do from a ministry perspective because I have spent two-thirds of my life doing volunteer ministries. While doing so, I have learned much about the *language of grounded faith.* At our church, we begin blend educating youth in faith with helping the local community. I am one of the team leaders for teens, so we also have a focus on the church's teaching on social justice. Our church has many outreach ministries supporting those in need locally and globally. We have taken teens and their parents to help at a daily ministry that feeds supper to over two hundred homeless and needy families. We also go to read or just be present with those at the local nursing home. Both teens and adults are in our Haiti ministry and a few go to Haiti to come back with amazing stories of love and gratitude. Before COVID, for many years we had a community garden supplying fresh produce along with parish members bringing non-perishable bags of food to the local food pantry. I spent almost ten years visiting various terminally ill people and found that they need someone to talk to before they go to heaven. Now as a grandparent and with friends my age who will be grandparents, I appreciate the opportunity to supply insight where I can.

We should bear in mind that a common denominator in ministry is that it is especially hard for new parents and grandparents to find time for anything additional. From a practical perspective, until they are settled back in, we cannot expect them to attend a new parent or grandparent ministry meeting. Depending on their situation that may mean a few months or a longer period. This means as people of faith, we should bring the values of peace, love, and hope within our specific faiths unconditionally and just in time to them. I have found that in one-on-one situations, it is not necessary for them to hear specific words of faith, but does it matter? One of my favorite quotes is from Saint Francis of Assisi, "Do all you can to preach the gospel and if necessary use words!" New parents and grandparents are in love all over again and are in tune without words with their children, and it runs over to those who are there for them. This simple realization has become obvious to me, given the thousands of hours of ministry and paying attention to those who need someone by their side.

From a ministry perspective, the best thing we can offer brand-new parents and grandparents is to humbly create some quality distraction-free time to be present just for them. Yes, it may be true that they may need your help holding their child while they wash the dishes. However, in their hearts and unspoken, what they need most is you as a cornerstone connecting them to a less hectic, stressful, and calmer reality. You can be that temporary conduit to their place of worship until they can do so again. When you visit a new parent or grandparent, you simply need to be full of God's peace and love. Spend some time to pray before your visit, and God will let you know if they need quiet or conversation. God will guide your actions, thoughts, or words to let a new parent or grandparent sense that you (and your faith community) are there for them. Your sacrifice will be returned to you via the spiritual rewards of doing so.

PS

I think and pray about what I have written and have additional thoughts. It dawned on me that I may not have emphasized that what I suggested works for me in my church and community. I am in a more rural community where there is a distance between houses and our church. Here people are open to having visitors to their homes. That may not be the case in other places. Also, this technique works best if the new parent or grandparent knows you well enough. The other caution I have is you need to be known as someone who is reserved with opinions, you do not reveal conversations, you are a good listener, can be trusted, and empathetic, and you have no problem with ensuring those who you would be visiting to leave their home as it is as you understand. Knowing how to visit takes practice and is a gift.

JOHN 16:21

When a woman is in labor, she has pain because her hour has come.
But when she gives birth to the child, she no longer remembers the anguish,
because of the joy that a human being has been born into the world.

Every worthwhile endeavor is strenuous and sometimes painful. Some people don't survive. Some endeavors never come to fruition.

But when all the pain and sweat and tears are gone and the thing is accomplished, that joy and success fill the center of our attention.

Do you teach your children this? Do you encourage them to keep trying, no matter how hard it is, or to give up, or to blame someone else for their failures? When they do something terrific, do you dwell on how hard it was and how you never thought they would do it? Or do you remind them that the success is theirs and was well worth the struggle?

Allow your children to fail at something. This will teach them that the mountains will not crumble into the seas if they are not perfect. This will also teach them that they are not entitled to things; they must work for them. Let them own their own failures, so they can learn how to succeed. Let them own their own successes, too, so they will learn the value of hard work and self-accomplishment.

SCARF

Scarves are wonderful things. They keep your neck warm and dangle mysteriously out of your coat. They add color to a bleary wintry day. They can be used to support and cheer on your favorite team. They can be made to match with mittens and sweaters and caps, or be a solitary accoutrement to one's wardrobe.

Scarves are simply very long rectangles, so one can make them using the ripple or the tunisian pattern, repeated double, single, or half double crochets. One can mix and match various stitches and broaden one's crochet horizons without committing oneself to a king-size afghan.

This pattern is a mixture of shells and chains. It makes up quickly and doesn't require keeping a paper pattern at one's fingertips constantly.

The length and width should keep the recipient in mind. It's very nice in solid colors, but I love the variegated, as it renders a lovely striped effect. It is worked along the sides – long-ways.

Just a note: I don't use fringe (I don't like fringe), but if you like it, put fringe on either end.

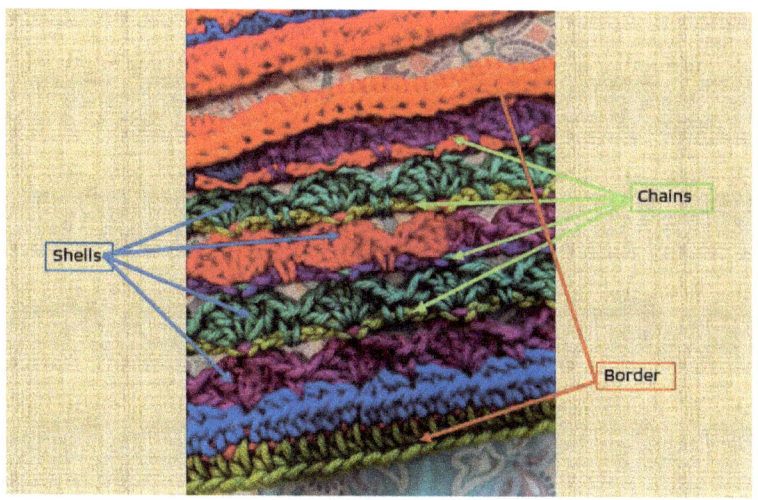

J hook
3-ply yarn

Chain in multiples of 5 until you have the desired length.
Row 1: Chain 2, turn. HDC in each stitch until the end of the row.

Row 2: Chain 3, turn, 2 DC in the base of your chain 3. [Skip 2, sc in next stitch, skip 2, 5 DC in next stitch.] Repeat [ ] until you are three stitches from the end. Skip 2. In the last stitch, 3 DC.

Row 3: Turn, [Chain 5. SC in both loops of the third DC of the next shell.] Repeat [ ] until the last stitch.

Row 4: Chain 3, turn, 2 DC in the base of your chain 3. [SC in the center of the chain, 5 DC in the stitch which was made at the top of the shell.] Repeat [ ] until you are at the last chain. SC in the center of that chain. In the last stitch, 3 DC.

Repeat rows 3 and 4 until your scarf is the desired width.

Last 2 rows:
A: Repeat Row 3
B: Turn, Chain 3, 4 DC in the first chain. 5 DC in each of the remaining chain groups.

Border:
In last stitch of row A, HDC, 2-chain, HDC. Turn the scarf so you are working along the short side. HDC in each stitch. In the corner, place [HDC, 2-chain, HDC]. Turn and work HDC along each stitch of the long side. In the corner, place [HDC, 2-chain, HDC]. Turn and work HDC along each stitch of the short side. In the corner, place [HDC, 2-chain, HDC]. Turn and work HDC along each stitch of the long side. Slip stitch to first HDC of first corner. Fasten off. Weave in tail.

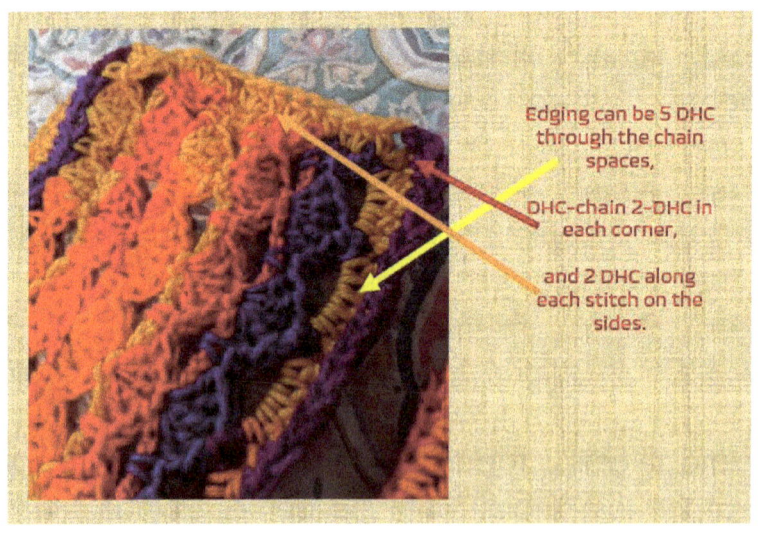

Edging can be 5 DHC through the chain spaces,

DHC-chain 2-DHC in each corner,

and 2 DHC along each stitch on the sides.

MATTHEW 19:13-14; MARK 10:13-15; LUKE 18:16-17

Then little children were brought to *Yeshua* so that He might lay hands upon them and pray.
Then the disciples rebuked those who brought them.
¹⁴ But *Yeshua* said, "Let the little children come to Me and do not hinder them, for the kingdom of heaven belongs to such as these."
(Matthew)

¹³ Now people were bringing little children to *Yeshua* so He might touch them, but the disciples rebuked those who brought them.
¹⁴ But when *Yeshua* saw this, He got angry.
He told them, "Let the little children come to Me! Do not hinder them, for the kingdom of God belongs to such as these.
¹⁵ Amen, I tell you, whoever does not receive the kingdom of God like a little child will never enter it!"
(Mark)

> [16] But *Yeshua* called for them, saying, "Let the little children come to Me and do not hinder them, for the kingdom of God belongs to such as these.
> [17] Amen, I tell you, whoever does not receive the kingdom of God like a little child will never enter it."
> (Luke)

The question persists – should your church, synagogue, or temple allow children in the sanctuary or should they be put into a children's nursery or self-contained unit during services.

Will children disrupt the service to the point that worship and healing cannot take place? Yes, if the children are not under the control of their parents.

Won't the sermon be too adult in concepts or content for the child to understand? Sometimes, but a healthy relationship between parent and child establishes communication and explanations by the parent when necessary and allows the child to ask questions.

The children would rather be playing with their friends than having to sit still for an hour. Yes, so would most adults, but learning how to behave in church, synagogue or temple is just as important as learning how to dine out in public, to dress appropriately for special occasions, and to respect societal rules. Beyond that, though, is the opportunity to teach a child how to pray, praise, and worship among friends.

MITTENS

The first time I tried to crochet mittens, I wound up with something monstrous. OK, I made several monstrous mitten-glove-basket-like things before I rewrote the pattern and made it my own.

I have to envision the finished product before the pattern actually makes sense to me. Music is similar – I read music, but I have to hear the tune, then I've got the soprano part nailed.

The secret to this pattern is that it begins on the pinky-edge of the hand. You make the palm side which continues onto the back side in each row, and once it is complete, you fold it at the fingertips and crochet up the edges, shifting the yarn beneath the thumb tip and the finger tips as you go along.

The pattern is done in this order: cuff (6 HDC), wrist (8 slip stitches), palm side (20 SC), finger tips (8 slip stitches), back of the hand (20 SC), wrist (8 slip stitches), and cuff (6 HDC). The 12 rows move the pattern from the heel of the hand to the thumb-side. The thumb is added in 4 rows, then the mitten edges are crocheted together.

Change hooks and yarn to match the age of the child or adult who will receive these mittens.

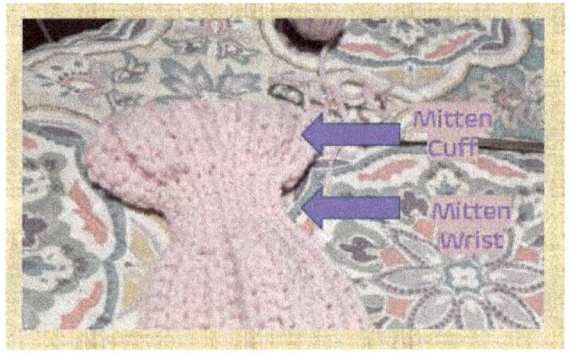

CARING FOR CHILDREN THROUGH CROCHET

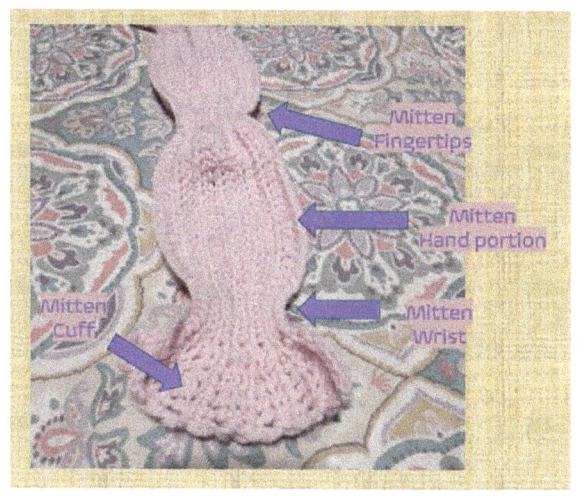

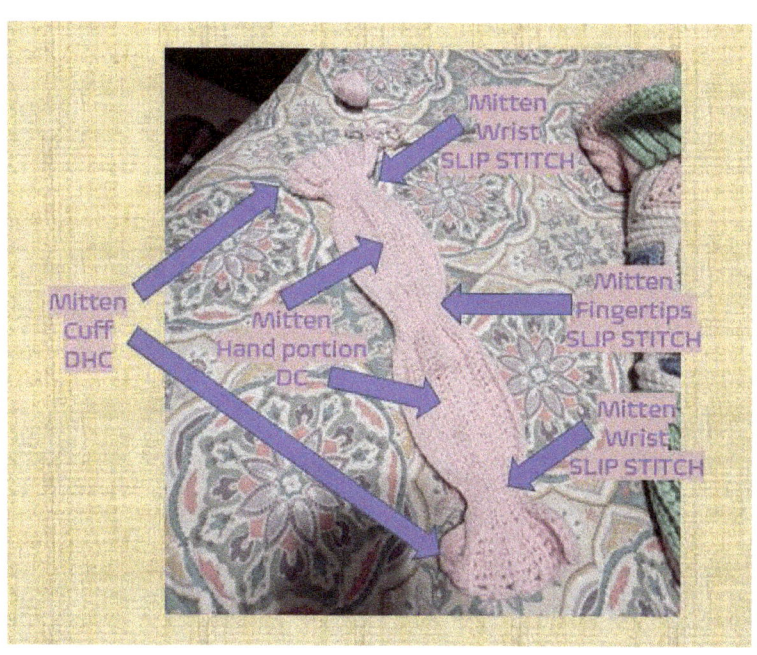

Chain 76, turn.

Row 1:
Chain 2 (counts as first HDC now and throughout). HDC in the third chain from the hook. Continue crocheting one stitch in each chain as stated: 4 DCH, 64 SC, 6 DCH. Turn.

Rows 2-12:
Chain 2 (counts as first HDC now and throughout)
5 HDC (cuff area)
8 slip stitches (wrist area)
20 SC (palm side)
8 slip stitches (finger tips)
20 sc (back of the hand)
8 slip stitch (wrist)
6 HDC (cuff) Turn

Row 13 (adding the thumb)
Chain 2 (counts as first HDC now and throughout)
5 HDC
8 slip stitch
8 sc
Chain 18 (be careful not to twist the chain)
Skip 32 stitches
8 sc
8 slip stitch
6 HDC

Rows 14-16

Chain 2 (counts as first HDC now and throughout)

5 HDC (cuff)

8 slip stitch (wrist)

15 sc, 4 slip stitch, 15 sc (thumb, thumb tip, thumb)

8 slip stitch (wrist)

6 HDC (cuff)

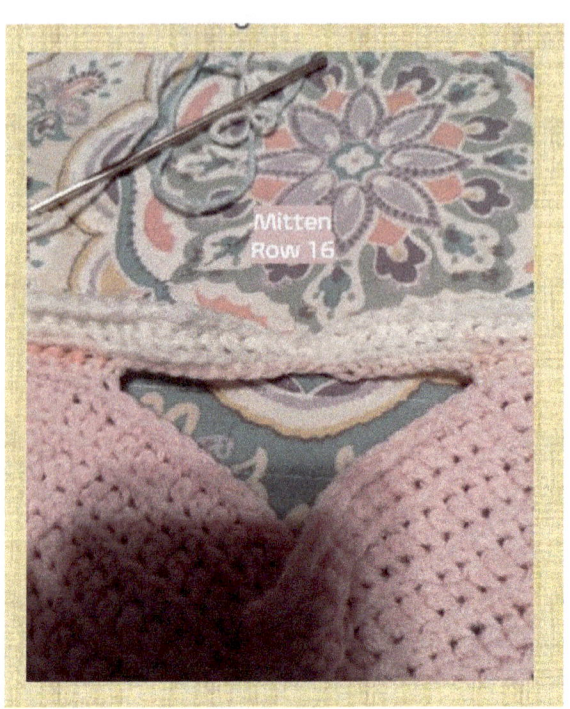

Mitten Row 16

Mitten Row 16

Edge

Wrong Side together

slip stitch together both sides up cuff, wrist, outer thumb

Lengthen the loop so it stretches across the top of thumb.

Slip stitch down the inside of the thumb and up the index side

Lengthen the loop so it stretches across the finger tips without pulling.

Move the hook to the other side of the hand and slip stitch down the heel of the hand, the wrist, and the cuff.

Frilly edge around the cuff if you wish. Fasten off, weave in, turn mitten outside in.

Make 2.

You may also use the mitten as a hand puppet by applying some of the finger puppet details.

MATTHEW 18:2-5; MARK 9:36-37

² And He called a child to Himself, set him in the midst of them, ³ and said, "Amen, I tell you, unless you turn and become like children, you shall never enter the kingdom of heaven.
⁴ Whoever then shall humble himself like this child, this one is the greatest in the kingdom of heaven.
⁵ And whoever welcomes one such child in My name, welcomes Me.
(Matthew)

³⁶ Taking a small child, He set him in the midst of them. And taking him in His arms, He said to them, ³⁷ "Whoever welcomes one of these children in My name, welcomes Me; and whoever welcomes Me, welcomes not Me but the One who sent Me."
(Mark)

What is a child actually like?

The definition of child is a human younger than puberty. Is Jesus saying that one should be without the sex hormones and drives that mark the entrance into adulthood?

Children love to play games and imagine wonderful things. Is Jesus saying that one should just have fun and play all day, imagining the unrealistic and never accomplishing anything of merit?

Children are trusting and innocent and have an intrinsic desire to be loved. According to Sanjana Gupta, those whose trust is betrayed grow into adults who "tend to avoid processing damaging behavior, normalize unhealthy behaviors, fabricate fantasies to compensate for painful memories, or even blame themselves."[5]

Those whose innocence is torn away never grow into completely whole adults. Authors of the 2018 article cited below stated, "The most commonly recorded diagnoses for trafficked children were post-traumatic stress disorder (PTSD) (22%) and affective disorders (22%). Records documented a high prevalence of physical violence (53%) and sexual violence (49%) among trafficked children."[6]

---

[5] Sanjana Gupta, Medically reviewed by Yolanda Renteria, LPC, "Betrayal Trauma—The Impact of Being Betrayed," May 4, 2023. Based on the 1991 Thesis by Jennifer Freyd, PhD, **Origin of the Betrayal Trauma Theory,** https://www.verywellmind.com/betrayal-trauma-causes-symptoms-impact-and-coping-5270361#.

[6] Livia Ottisova, Patrick Smith, Hitesh Shetty, Daniel Stahl, Johnny

Those who are not supplied with love and affection develop Reactive Attachment Disorder. Dr. Juhi Mehrotra stated, "As the child grows older he/she may develop either inhibited or disinhibited behavioral symptoms.

- Inhibited: The child is withdrawn, does not react to respond, and is emotionally detached.
- Disinhibited: The child shows indiscriminate sociability, seeks attention from everyone and acts much younger than his/her age."[7]

Jesus said to be childlike – innocent, trusting, loving, and to accept and help maintain those who are innocent, trusting, and loving. Be the kind of parent or grandparent who ensures the continuance of innocence, trust, and love for those in your charge.

Downs, Sian Oram, Psychological consequences of child trafficking: An historical cohort study of trafficked children in contact with secondary mental health services, Published: March 8, 2018, https://doi.org/10.1371/journal.pone.0192321.

[7] Dr. Juhi Mehrotra, MD Pediatrics, "Reactive Attachment Disorder," MSN, https://www.msn.com/en-us/health/condition/reactive-attachment-disorder?source=bing_condition.

THE INNOCENT BYSTANDERS OF DOMESTIC VIOLENCE / INTIMATE PARTNER VIOLENCE EXPOSURE

By Rita Langdale, LCSW, RD

Domestic violence (DV), also known as intimate partner violence (IPV), has a ripple effect on the entire family, not just the targeted victim. The term IPV will be used here on out. IPV is defined by the Center for Disease Control and Prevention (CDC) as abuse that takes place in romantic relationships and includes physical, sexual, stalking, and psychological aggression (CDC, Oct 2022). It is estimated that 41% of women (16 million) and 26% (11 million) of men experience IPV during their lifetime. These statistics are believed to be underestimated as abuse often goes unreported for fear of additional abuse. According to the National Coalition Against Domestic Violence (NCADV, 2021) 1 in 15 children annually are exposed to IPV. An estimated 10 - 15 million children in the U.S. have witnessed at least one occurrence of IPV in the last year and 7 million live in homes where IPV is a regular occurrence (*Futures without Violence,* 2014). IPV is considered an epidemic (Center for Disease Control & Prevention, 2021) and those working with children need to be vigilant when working with children who have been exposed to IPV.

When ministering to children and families that have experienced IPV it is imperative to understand the effects of this exposure. Too often children are labeled as 'bad' because they exhibit behaviors that can be aggressive. When children are labeled as 'bad' they tend to live up to that behavior versus when an adult shows them compassion the child is more likely to be reachable and redirectable. I am not saying that unruly behaviors should not be addressed, I am saying we need to understand that the behavior is likely an outlet for the trauma they are enduring when exposed to IPV. Children who are exposed to IPV, or any trauma for that matter, are often unable to regulate emotions. This inability to regulate emotions is a typical trademark of IPV exposure and these children need to be taught how to regulate emotions. Children tend to exhibit either internalizing or externalizing behaviors or a combination of both. Internalizing behaviors include such things as depression, anxiety, and self-harm behaviors which include suicidal ideations, cutting, and eating disorders. Externalizing behaviors include aggression, oppositional defiant behaviors, and criminal acts (Rizvi & Najam, 2014; Spinazzola et al., 2014). When left untreated the effects of IPV exposure can have lasting mental and physical consequences including obesity, diabetes, cardiovascular disease, insomnia, chronic depression, and social anxiety (Cage et al., 2021;

Dodaj, 2020). These effects are seen well into adulthood. IVP exposure can also lead to the child later being a victim of IPV or the aggressor in relationships; this is known as transgenerational trauma. The concept is out of the scope of this writing; however, it is when the effects of trauma are passed down from one generation to the next (Choi et al. 2020).

What can you do to have a positive impact on the lives of these children? For starts showing kindness, compassion, and genuine concern and love for every child, even the challenging ones.

When working with children and families who have experienced IPV it is critical to encourage mental health counseling. Counseling with a qualified mental health professional has been shown to decrease internalizing and externalizing behaviors and teach children to regulate emotions in a healthy manner. When mental health counseling is encouraged, it continues to break the stigma still attached to seeking mental health services. We need to talk about the importance of mental health counseling, just as much as we talk about seeing a medical physician for a physical illness. Additionally, those that work with children and their families need to advocate for community resources and ensure that families have access to these services. When we encourage counseling and ensure children have access to these services, we begin to break the chains of transgenerational trauma and we set these children up for successful and productive lives. Thank you for all that you do for the children of your community.

References

Cage, J., Kobulsky, J. M., McKinney, S. J., Holmes, M. R., Berg, K. A., Bender, A. E., & Kemmerer, A. (2021). The effect of exposure to intimate partner violence on children's academic functioning: A systematic review of the literature. *Journal of Family Violence.* https://doi.org/10.1007/s10896-021-00314-0

Center for Disease Control & Prevention (2021) *Intimate Partner Violence.* https://www.cdc.gov/violenceprevention/intimatepartnerviolence/fastfact.html

Choi, K. R., Stewart, T., Fein, E., McCreary, M., Kenan, K. N., Davies, J. D., Naureckas, S., & Zima, B. T. (2020). The impact of attachment-disrupting adverse childhood experiences on child behavioral health. *The Journal of Pediatrics, 221*, 224–229. https://doi.org/10.1016/j.jpeds.2020.03.006

Dodaj, A. (2020). Children witnessing domestic violence. *Journal of Children's Services.* 15(3),161-174. https://doi.org/10.1108/jcs-04-2019-0023

Futures without Violence. (July 15, 2014) *The Facts on Children's Exposure to Intimate Partner Violence.* https://www.futureswithoutviolence.org/the-facts-on-childrens-exposure-to-intimate-partner-violence/

National Center for Injury Prevention and Control, Division of Violence Prevention. (2022, October 11). *Preventing intimate partner violence.* Centers for Disease Control and Prevention. https://www.cdc.gov/violenceprevention/intimatepartnerviolence/fastfact.html

National Coalition Against Domestic Violence. (2021). *Statistics.* NCADV. https://ncadv.org/statistics

Rizvi, S. F. I. & Najam, N. (2014). Parental psychological abuse and mental health problems in adolescents. *Pakistan Journal of Medical Sciences, 30*(2). https://doi.org/10.12669/pjms.302.4593

Spinazzola, J., Hodgdon, H., Liang, L.-J., Ford, J. D., Layne, C. M., Pynoos, R., Briggs, E. C., Stolbach, B., & Kisiel, C.

(2014). Unseen wounds: The contribution of psychological maltreatment to child and adolescent mental health and risk outcomes. *Psychological Trauma: Theory, Research, Practice, and Policy, 6*(Suppl 1), S18–S28. https://doi.org/10.1037/a0037766

About Rita Langdale

Foundress of **Her Voice in the Darkness** **(https://hervoiceinthedarkness.com/)**

Rita is a Licensed Clinical Social Worker (LCSW) and a Registered Dietitian (RD). **Her Voice in the Darkness** has a two-fold reason for being formed. The first reason came out of a personal experience with psychological (emotional and verbal) abuse behind closed doors: being in the church environment added to the forced silence disguised as submission. After seven years in an abusive marriage, Rita was able to break the silence. It became her passion to be the voice for those not yet able to speak of the abuse they are enduring. The second reason is that while in private practice she witnessed firsthand how unspoken social norms force women to isolate and struggle mentally and emotionally in silence. She works with female clients who often come out of childhood with a feeling of not being good enough. This feeling results in women not being authentically themselves. It also results in women getting into relationships that are abusive because they lack self-esteem and the confidence to live up to their true calling.

Her voice in the darkness is dedicated to all the women whose voices have been silenced under unspoken social norms and within the church culture disguised as submission. May you reclaim your voice so that generations to come do not have to endure oppression.

ACTS 2:39

For the promise is for you and your children, and for all who are far away—
as many as *ADONAI* our God calls to Himself.

A promise to a child is different from a promise to an adult. Or is it? Did we view promises differently when we were children, learning along the years that some promises were never meant to be kept?

When you make a promise to your child, do you keep it? Does your child keep his or her promises to you?

That feeling of betrayal as a child, when someone we loved broke a promise, is something we never forget. It haunts us every time someone else gives us a promise.

But the promise of God – to keep us as His people and shelter us in His arms for all eternity – is a promise which will never be broken. And this is not just a promise for a special few, but for you and for your children, for foreigners and for everyone who believes in God.

CROCHETED PLASTIC HANGERS

By now, you probably have a dozen partially used balls of yarn from these projects. Also, just so you know, neither Salvation Army nor the Goodwill will accept coathangers as donations. So, here is a simple and creative way to deal with both abundances.

According to *Hanger Guide*, "Padded hangers are a type of hanger that has extra padding on the shoulders in order to support the weight of your clothes better. While they are more expensive than regular hangers, they can help to prolong the life of your clothes by preventing them from stretching out or becoming misshapen."[8]

Children's clothes wear out soon enough; putting them on padded hangers might help extend the life of their clothes, at least until they outgrow them. Plus, a dozen of these beauties tied together with a bow would make a lovely gift.

Since you have been using 100% acrylic yarn for this book, I won't have to warn you not to use colored cotton or wool, and the color might fade onto the clothes.

Use a J or K hook. Place the plastic hanger so the neck is facing your left. It is easiest to work in the apex (the corner). Place your first stitch – a slip stitch, then use HDC and work your way around the hanger until the entire triangle is covered. Slip stitch into the first stitch and tie off. Then tie the two ends together in a square knot. If you wish, you may also tie a ribbon at the base of the hanger neck to cover your knot.

You may also try DC or SC, or a mixture to develop interesting textures. If the SC is too tight, use a larger hook. Try different yarns, too. Pictured are Lion Brand and Red Heart yarns; what a difference the weight makes! You may continue tying one end of yarn to the next (square knot and weave in the ends) or use only one yarn color per hangers. The choice is yours. Enjoy!

---

[8] Admin, "What Are Padded Hangers For?" *Hanger Guide*, September 27, 2022, https://hangersguide.com/what-are-padded-hangers-for/

CARING FOR CHILDREN THROUGH CROCHET

It's easiest to work in the corner and shift the stitches along the bottom edge and up to the neck.

I THESSALONIANS 2:5-8

⁵ For as you know and God is witness, we never came with a word of flattery or a motive of greed— ⁶ or seeking glory from people, whether from you or from others, ⁷ even though we could have thrown our weight around as emissaries of Messiah.
Rather, we proved to be infants among you. Like a nursing mother cherishes her children, ⁸ in this way we were yearning for you.
We were delighted to share with you not only the Good News of God but also our very souls, because you had become dear to us.

Some parents just know what to do. They march into a situation and take over. Anyone who doesn't agree with them is obviously misinformed and/or wrong. They stomp on a few toes, but those probably needed to be stepped on anyway. They get the job done and everyone seems to be pleased with the result. Or at least, no one says anything in opposition; but there is very little praise, either.

If you are a parent like that, you will begin to notice your child cringing whenever you say you are going to go with them to an activity. Eventually, he or she will resent you attending anything, and their friends will treat them hatefully because they have picked up how you have treated their parents. You will find yourself getting things done, but not enjoying it.

Paul's advice in 1 Thessalonians is to be gentle. Treat others the way you would treat your own nursing infant. Care for them, listen to them, yearn for them to accomplish things. Share your "very soul" with them. Your children and their friends and their friends' parents will be delighted with your attendance and direction.

HUGGABLE TOYS

One of the most calming activities for an anxious child is hugging something soft and cuddly. As you minister to children who have suffered loss, trauma, and even normal life-events, having a huggable stuffed animal available is a great gift. Your group can make these by the dozens and donate them to your local police and sheriff offices as well as emergency rooms. Keep a few by the back pews to give to children who are staying in the church, synagogue, or temple during services.

The following pattern is for a basic 4-appendaged, plump bodied, spherical head type doll, with or without tail. You can add ears: triangular for a cat, folded down for a puppy, elongated for a bunny, wing-shaped for an elephant; the possibilities are endless. You can make the tail straight, curled, fluffy, or short by changing the yarn and the length of the tail.

Most patterns call for safety eyes, but those just make me nervous. Children bite, chew, and suck on things all the time. I would suggest you embroider the eyes and other facial features.

Remember to use washable acrylic yarn and embroidery thread as well as washable, 100% hypoallergenic stuffing material.

You'll need a stitch marker; H, G, or F crochet hooks, thread and yarn embroidery needles; stuffing, and doll-sized clothing and other articles (hats, scarves, purses, etc.) that you can add to your doll. Whenever you fasten off, allow a long piece of yarn as the tail; you'll be using those to crochet your body parts together. You can specifically choose color-coordinated or life-like yarn, or use leftovers to render a patchwork effect.

The final size is dependent on the size of your stitches and the number of rows you use. Add rows for larger dolls or keep it small as stated.

LIMBS (make 4)

Chain 3, slip stitch into first chain to form ring, chain 1. 6 SC inside the circle.

Row 1: Work in both loops now and throughout. Work 2 sc in each stitch. Place your stitch marker here and move it up with each row.

Rows 2 and 3: SC in each stitch around

Row 4: [SC in next 2 stitches, sc2tog] repeat around to marker

Row 5: SC in each stitch around

Repeat row 5 until the limb is the length you wish. The legs are usually longer than the arms. Fill with fiberfill to this point.

Row 6: [SC in next stitch, SC2tog in next stitch] Repeat around to marker.

The photo sample has the arms 7 rows long and the legs 10 rows long.

Last Row: HDC in each stitch around. Fasten off with long tail. Stuff firmly with fiberfill.

TAIL

Chain 3, slip stitch into first chain to form ring, chain 1. 6 SC inside the circle.

HDC in each stitch until the tail is the desired length. Use fringe yarn for fluffy tails, fuzzy yarn for fuzzy tails, etc. It should be tight enough not to need fiberfill, but you can use a dowl to help lightly stuff it if you wish. Chain 1. Press sides together. SC in the 3 paired stitches, closing the top of the tail. Fasten off and leave long tail of yarn.

HEAD

Chain 3, slip stitch into first chain to form ring, Chain 1. 6 SC inside the circle.

Row 1: Work in both loops now and throughout. Work 2 sc in each stitch. Place your stitch marker here and move it up with each row.

Row 2: [SC in stitch, 2 SC in next stitch] repeat around to marker.

Row 3: [SC in stitch, SC in next stitch, 2 SC in next stitch] repeat around to marker.

Row 4: [SC in stitch, SC in next stitch, SC in next stitch, 2 SC in next stitch] repeat around to marker.

Row 5: [SC in each of next 4 stitches, 2 SC in next stitch] repeat around to marker.

Row 6: : [SC in each of next 5 stitches, 2 SC in next stitch] repeat around to marker.

Row 7: SC in each of next stitches around to marker. (42 stitches)

Rows 8-16: Repeat Row 7

Embroider eyes 7 stitches apart between rows 13 and 14. If you don't want to stop here, you can put in Clones Knots – one for each eye – and keep crocheting around. (See instructions at the end of this article.)

Row 17: [SC in each of next 5 stitches, sc2tog in next stitch] repeat around to marker.

Row 18: [SC in each of next 4 stitches, sc2tog in next stitch] repeat around to marker.

Row 19: [SC in each of next 3 stitches, sc2tog in next stitch] repeat around to marker.

Row 20: [SC in each of next 2 stitches, sc2tog in next stitch] repeat around to marker. (18 stitches).

Fill the head firmly with fiberfill, making sure that you don't stretch the stiches apart, showing the fill.

BODY

The body continues from the neck of the head and as you get to the appropriate places, you will crochet in the appendages. Use the yarn-tail and the presently used yarn at the same time; thus doubling with strengthen the attachments so they are less likely to be pulled apart.

Row 1: Turn the head upside down and work in the neck opening. Slip stitch to your marker (the last stitch made in the head), chain 1. Use the tail piece along with your yarn. SC in each stitch around. (move marker up as you go.)

Row 2: Work 2 sc in each stitch.

Row 3: [SC in stitch, 2 SC in next stitch] repeat around to marker.

Row 4: [SC in stitch, SC in next stitch, 2 SC in next stitch] repeat around to marker.

Row 5: [SC in next 3 stitches, 2 SC in next stitch] repeat around to marker.

Row 6: Place the arms where they should be. As you SC in each stitch around, combine the yarn-tail with your yarn and crochet the top three stitches of the limb on the front side of the body.

Row 7: SC around until you reach the arms. SC2tog for each of the side stitches of the arms, slip across and allow slack to reach the other side of the arm, SC around.

Row 8: SC around until you reach the arms. Crochet the back three stitches of the arms on the backside of the body, using the yarn-tail to double the yarn and work wrong sides together, SC around.

Row 9: [SC in each of next 3 stitches, 2 SC in next stitch] repeat around to marker.

Row 10: SC in each stitch around

Head & Shoulders Row 10

Row 11: [SC in each of next 4 stitches, 2 SC in next stitch] repeat around to marker.

Row 12: SC in each stitch around

Row 13: [SC in each of next 5 stitches, 2 SC in next stitch] repeat around to marker.

Rows 14-16: SC around. (and as many rows as you wish to obtain the length of the body).

Row 17: [SC in each of next 5 stitches, SC2-tog in next stitch] repeat around to marker.

Row 18: [SC in each of next 4 stitches, SC2-tog in next stitch] repeat around to marker.

Row 19: [SC in each of next 3 stitches, SC2-tog in next stitch] repeat around to marker.

Rows 20-22: SC around.

Row 23: Place the tail where it should be. As you SC in each stitch around, crochet in the three stitches of the tail, using the yarn-tail to double the yarn and work right sides together. Leave the yarn-tail behind to be picked up on the next row.

Stuff body firmly, adding a little more so that the abundance will even out into the final rows.

Rows 24-26: Place the legs where they should be.

Row 24: As you SC in each stitch around, combine the yarn-tail with your yarn and crochet the top three stitches of the limb on the front side of the body.

Row 25: SC around until you reach the legs. SC2tog for each of the side stitches of the legs, slip across and allow slack to reach the other side of the arm, SC around.

Row 26: SC around until you reach the legs. Crochet the back three stitches of the legs on the backside of the body, using the yarn-tail to double the yarn and work wrong sides together, SC around.

Row 27-end: In the space between the legs and tail, crochet 2 together around until the space is closed. This allows a flat surface for the doll to sit upon. Fasten off. Weave tail in.

Back View. Note the placement of the tail and legs and the flat, final stitches which closed the body.

Embroider and embellish as you see fit. Add ears, hair, fur, whiskers, a nose, eyelashes, mouth, etc.

Your huggable toy is ready to have you add specific features: hair or hat, bow or buttons, shirt or skirt, etc.

CLONES KNOT

A clones knot was developed in Irish Lace to strengthen the chains between the motifs. It was designed in Clones, Ireland (hence the name). This is where a Boye hook comes into its true glory.

Chain 1. Hold the end of your hook with your crochet hand and with the other hand, the chain in the center of the thumb shape on the hook. Move your hook under the yarn, then twirl the hook 180 degrees counter clock wise, and then loop under the yarn and twirl the hook back - clockwise – 180 degrees. Keep the loops firm but not tight. Keep the loops centered on the thumb space of the hook. Repeat : under the yarn and twirl counterclockwise 180 degrees, the under the yarn and twirl clockwise 180 degrees. Do this 8 times for sports yarn, 12 times for fingering yarn, 18 times for thread yarn.
Then, continue to hold the chain in one hand, slip the loops of yarn up and down the hook shaft, twirling the thumb space to help open the cocoon of yarn slightly. When it slides easily, yarn over and pull through the entire cocoon. Yarn over, chain and pull tight. Clones knot completed. Chain again, then continue your crochet pattern.

Please do not be discouraged if you have trouble with this stitch. It is difficult to learn, but once learned, it is so much fun.

1 JOHN 3:1-2

See how glorious a love the Father has given us, that we should be called God's children—and so we are! The reason the world does not know us is that it did not know Him. ² Loved ones, now we are God's children; and it has not yet been revealed what we will be. But we do know that when it's revealed, we shall be like Him, because we will see Him just as He is.

Have you ever been a guest at a family reunion? You only know the one person who invited you – who hasn't shown up yet, but everyone there knows everyone there – except you. They try to recognize you and connect you with a family line, but once they understand you are a stranger, they smile vacantly and walk away.

Then, your friend walks in and smiles at you. He embraces you and everyone welcomes him and you! Then, because you belong to him, you belong to them!

How do your children feel when they are with you and your friends? Are they strangers, or are they welcomed because you include them?

MINISTERING TO CHILDREN THROUGH CROCHET

by Evelyn Rainey

There are so many different ways to use crochet to minister to children. Here are just a few ways to use each item.

Caps – October is National Anti-Bullying month in most public schools. Blue caps are the symbol of anti-bullying. Offer blue caps to your local elementary school students to support their stand against bullying.

Kimono, caps, diaper cover – for premature babies, the only item of clothing they can wear in the hospital are caps – which are life-saving, and then later, diaper covers and kimonos. They must be hypoallergenic (cotton or acrylic) and small enough to fit a 2-6 pound baby. Offer them to your local OBGYN facilities or hospitals.

Booties, caps, afghan, diaper cover, kimono – for any baby, this combination is the perfect gift. Offer these sets to your local teen parent programs (contact them through your public school system). Also, set up a policy to gift this set to each newborn who is in your church, synagogue, or temple.

Breast-Feeding Modesty Shawl - this in and by itself is a wonderful gift to any nursing mother. Offer them to your local or national lactation groups (see the internet for courses).

Button covers, egg rattles, huggable toys, finger puppets, dragon capes, crocheted hangers – offer these to foster children through your local agency.

Huggable toys – have a basket of them by the ushers to give one to each new child who comes into your service. They should then be allowed to take it home. You can also offer them to your local emergency rooms and law enforcement agencies.

Caps, mittens, scarf – perfect set to give to children who may not have enough warm clothing. Offer them through your local schools and food kitchens. Tuck them into the Kids Pack meals just as the weather turns chilly.

Egg rattles – allow children to use them during the services – to shake during the hymns and to play with during the sermons (check with your minister first). You can also offer these to adults for use during the music, too. For years, I included them with a local church's annual Operation Christmas Child boxes (but do not use beans as the rattles if you are going to send them overseas).

As you see, you will not want to just make one thing to give away. Everything works as sets, and each set can be personalized and specific to the recipient. Have your Prayer Shawl group work together so that the person who makes the best mittens can spend her time making mittens while the person who enjoys making afghans or finger puppets or dragon capes can do that, and the set of crocheters can agree on matching colors and sizes.

I JOHN 3:18

Children, let us not love with word or talk, but in deed and truth!

Talk is cheap.

Saying that one day, you will feed the hungry, or clothe the naked, or visit the sick, or welcome the stranger, or contact a prisoner, is cheap. But **doing** these things – giving canned foods to the food ministry, taking all your gently-used clothes to the Salvation Army, or putting together activity baskets and sitting with those who are in the hospital or are homebound, or helping with the prison ministry, these are acts of love in deed and in truth.

DRAGON CAPE

The body of this cape is a granny square of 17 rows. Use colors that are dragonish, either several different colors or a variegated skein or two, or a mixture of solid and variegated. There are books and articles about which dragon is which color and what powers those dragons have, etc. Have fun and create your own unique dragons.

Make the pieces in this order:
Body
Tail
Hands (2)
Forehead
Fringe
Spine

Basic body:
Chain 3, join in circle
First row inside the circle:
Chain two (counts as launch stitch = one double crochet)
2 DC inside circle
Chain 2
3 DC inside circle
(one **corner** made)
Chain 1
3 DC, chain 2, 3 DC
Chain 1

3 DC, chain 2, 3 DC
Chain 1
3 DC, chain 2, 3 DC
Chain 1
Slip stitch to first chain.

Row 2:
Chain 3
(2 DC, chain 2, 3 DC) inside first chain-2 space (aka corner)
Chain 1

3 DC in chain 1 space
Chain 1

3 DC, chain 2, 3 DC in next chain-2 space (2nd corner)
Chain 1

3 DC in chain 1 space
Chain 1

3 DC, chain 2, 3 DC in next chain-2 space (3rd corner)
Chain 1

3 DC in chain 1 space
Chain 1

3 DC, chain 2, 3 DC in next chain-2 space (4th corner)
Chain 1
Slip Stitch to chain 3 space

Rows 4-17
Continue each row with chain 3 after the slip stitch. Put [3DC - chain 2 - 3DC] in each corner. Chain 1 between each side clump of 3DC in each chain 1 space.

Fasten off and weave in yarn.

TAIL:
The tail can be made several different ways. I do something different each time. I have included the basic pattern, but be fearless and adapt it as you see fit.

Start 9 stitches from the corner. DC in each stitch. (2DC, chain 2, 2DC) in the corner. DC for 9 more stitches. Chain 3 and turn. Continue working 5 rows.
Row 6: Slip stitch 5 stitches, DC to corner, (2DC, chain 2, 2DC) in the corner. DC to 5 stitches from the end of Row 5. Chain 3 and turn.
Repeat for rows 7-10: 1 DC in each stitch and (2DC, chain 2, 2DC) in the corner, followed by DC in each stitch. Chain 3, turn.
Row 11: Slip stitch 7 stitches, DC to corner, (2DC, chain 2, 2DC) in the corner. DC to 7 stitches from the end of Row 5. Chain 3 and turn.
Repeat for rows 12-15: 1 DC in each stitch and (2DC, chain 2, 2DC) in the corner, followed by DC in each stitch. Chain 3, turn.
Row 16: Slip stitch 9 stitches, DC to corner, (2DC, chain 2, 2DC) in the corner. DC to 9 stitches from the end of Row 15. Chain 3 and turn.

Repeat for rows 17-20: Slip stitch 3 stitches, DC to corner, (2DC, chain 2, 2DC) in the corner. DC to 3 stitches from the end of previous row. Chain 3 and turn. This should taper the tail until it is 3 stitches wide. Fasten off and weave in.

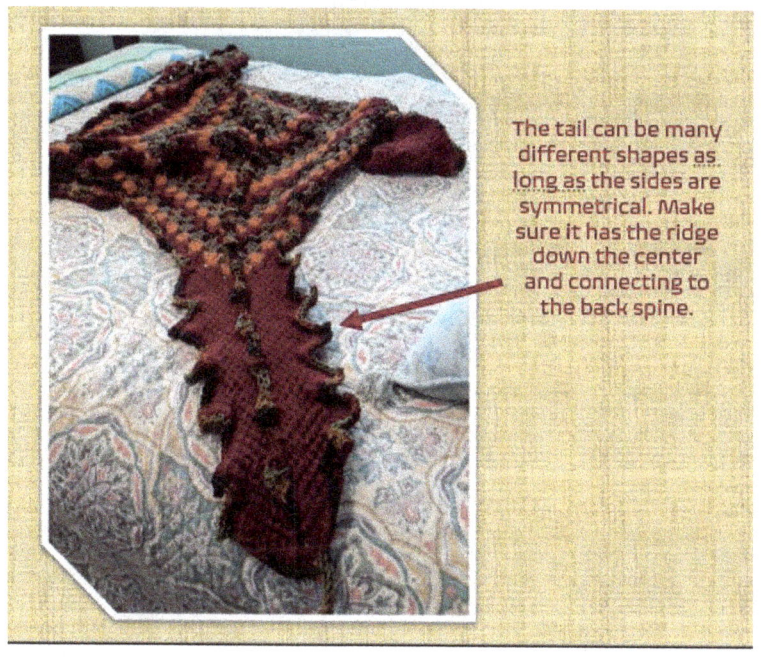

The tail can be many different shapes as long as the sides are symmetrical. Make sure it has the ridge down the center and connecting to the back spine.

Hands: Use the pattern for the shawls to make 2 triangles which are 4 rows wide.

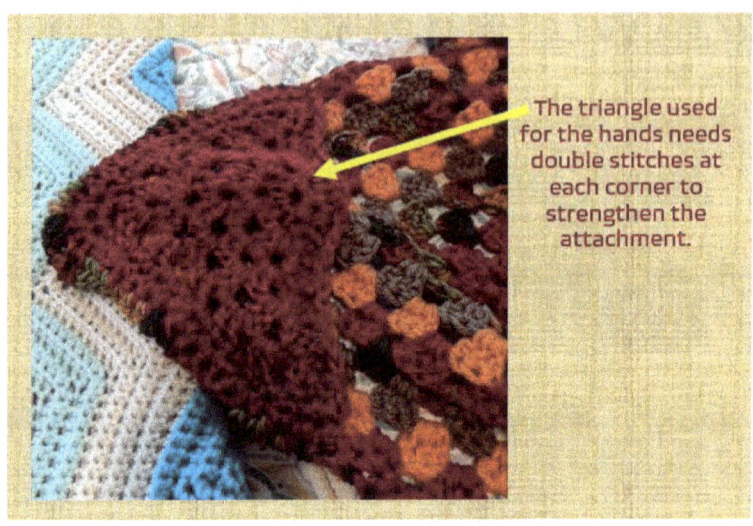

The triangle used for the hands needs double stitches at each corner to strengthen the attachment.

Forehead: Use the pattern for the shawls to make 1 triangle which is 5 rows wide.

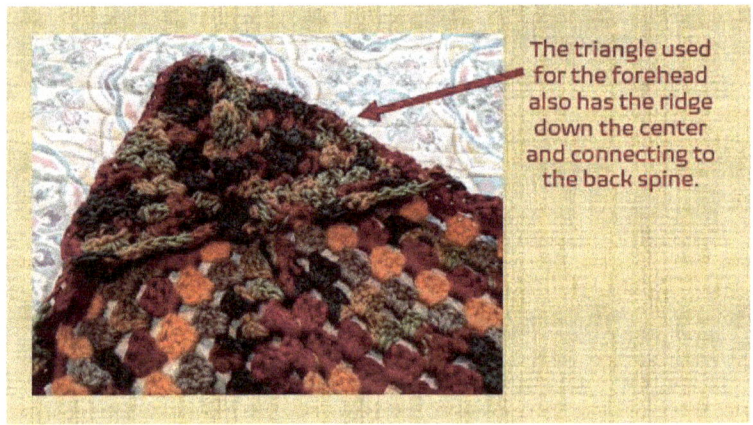

The triangle used for the forehead also has the ridge down the center and connecting to the back spine.

Fringe/Edge: First row, SC in each stitch around the border, using this process to bind the hands and the forehead to the body. In each corner, put (SC, chain 2, SC). Second row, repeat this pattern (SC, HDC, DCH, DC, DC, [TC, chain 2, TC] in one stitch, DC, DC, HDC, HDC, SC), adjusting when you get to corners so that you wind up with the SC at the apex. Put three SC in each corner.

The spine is the most fun thing to crochet on this pattern. It starts as a 5 chain with SC attaching it to the corners of the diagonal square. Start at the front of the forehead, over the head, down the back and continue to the tip of the tail. Then turn and put these stitches in every other 5-chain: SC, HDC, DC, TC, chain 2, TC, DC, HDC, SC. Slip stitch in the center of the next 5-chain.

1 JOHN 5:2

We know that we love God's children by this—when we love God and obey His commandments.

I am often wary of businesses which claim to be Christian-owned. I know this is a huge and profitable marketing label. But the way I am treated by the business tells me far more about that person's religion than the painted letters on his sign.

Children know your religion by the way you treat them, too. Not by taking them to church and youth group and making them memorize Scriptures or the Torah. They know by how you love them.

3 JOHN 1:4

I have no greater joy than this—to hear that my children are walking in the truth.

Parents love to brag about their children. That's good and natural and I encourage it. But I also hope that one of the things you can brag about is that your child is also a child of God. And I hope they are just as pleased and proud to say that you are also a child of God.

No greater joy, to know your children will be with you on earth and in heaven.

THE BENEDICTION

Numbers 6:24-26

[24] The LORD bless you, and keep you:

[25] The LORD make His face shine upon you,

and be gracious unto you:

[26] The LORD lift up His countenance upon you

and give you peace.

ABOUT CREATIVE CROCHET PATTERNS

Strive to be faithful to that to which God has called you.

St. Angela Merici

Foundress of the Ursaline Sisters

To crochet, one takes a piece of yarn (or thread, grass, string, ribbon, etc.) and a hooked stick and creates a three-dimensional item.

The Vikings from 800-1066 CE did a similar art called *nalbinding*. Also similar is *shepherd's knitting* as found in Scotland, Sweden, Norway, Iceland, Estonia, Romania, the Balkans, and the British Isles. Another similar needlework was *pjoining* as found in Denmark. The etymology of the word *crochet* also spans history: the Norse word *krokr* (hook), the German word *croc* (hook) and French word *crochet* (small hook or canine tooth) became established as the word for this needlecraft in 1846; the word *crochet-needle* was established in 1848, and *crochet-hook* in 1849, followed by the word *crochet-work* in 1856. (However, my laptop dictionary still refuses to recognize the noun *crocheter* today.)

The history of crochet (before it was named crochet) stretches back to the early 1700's from France in the form of *tambour*. It was in France that the embroidery fabric was abandoned and the stitches were done "in the air" with hooks. In France, this new crochet was recognized as a cheap substitute for French lace. (When I say *cheap*, please realize that people were imprisoned and transported for life to Australia and/or the New World for stealing as little as 12 inches of French lace.) Eventually, as the Potato Famine ravaged Ireland, crochet was introduced by the Urseline nuns of France (who also expanded into Canada and New Orleans in the early 1700's and are still going strong internationally – see https://www.osucentral.org/) as a way for whole villages and clans to produce cheap lace and stave off starvation. This technique was known as Irish Lace and the Clones Knot (see this book page 174 for instructions) was an original structure developed in Clones, Ireland to help strengthen the chains between the motifs. The structure (pattern) of each motif was a closely held secret, created and perfected by individual members of the clan, because such intricate patterns were what set each clan's Irish lace apart from other clans. The patterns were shared verbally between friends and family, occasionally sewn into soft paper books which were cherished and protected. Shared crochet patterns often left out a particular stitch – on purpose or not. (I think some of us can understand this behavior. My Great-aunt Ida occasionally left out a key ingredient in her coveted recipes – so that no one could make that dish "quite like Ida did.") And what one crocheter meant by one stitch was often mistaken for a different stitch by someone else. There was no true uniformity in crochet. Over the centuries, crochet stitches, procedures, and patterns have become more standardized, although there is still the difference between English and American stitches (same names, different numbers of loops) and no one launches their hook in the same manner as anyone else.

Written crochet patterns did not officially come into being until 1824 in the Dutch magazine *Penelope*. Then in 1851, crochet was permanently established as a needlecraft entry in the *Great Exhibition in London;* a prize was given for a crocheted lace dress created by Mlle Eleonore Riego de la Branchardiere. She then went on to publish reproducible patterns and crochet became firmly established in the lives of Victorian women.

When I began to crochet, I learned by sitting next to someone and watching her. I would repeat her motions, and with some gentle redirections, soon was able to create caps, blankets, and various other items by myself. They were not *exact* replicas of the teachers' items – they were *creative* representatives of what I wanted to make. And that's how I teach my students – by example and demonstration.

I tried to follow written patterns, but was content with taking charge of their ideas and making them my own. Quite honestly, written patterns slowed me down, confused me, and kept me chained to the book or magazine. It was often my habit to examine the picture in great detail, scan over the written codes, and then make the item as I saw fit. Along the way, I learned to adjust the size of my hooks to fit the yarn and the weight of my yarns to fit the final project. I learned to change a basic doll to fit the child's favorite animal, or the size of a sweater to fit a child, youth, or adult as needed. *I thought everyone crocheted this way.*

I would occasionally write down my "patterns" and refer back to them as needed, tweaking, changing, and correcting them along the way. My first Prayer Shawl Ministry book – **Woven Prayers** – was a collection of such patterns, and it was to my great surprise when other firmly established crochet artists could not follow my patterns. I tried to be much more precise in this book, but it is just fine with me if you do not follow my instructions letter by letter. These patterns are just basic designs which are intended to be tweaked, added to, corrected, expanded upon, and embellished. I want you to make each item your own. Change what you want to change. As with the first Irish motifs, if your butterfly and my butterfly look like butterflies, I will be very happy, and I hope that you are, too. My friend Mark Jaskolka assured me that being a creative crocheter is just fine. (Thank you, Mark!)

Please feel free to contact me for assistance – with your prayer shawl ministries and with your crochet.

ABOUT THE AUTHOR

Evelyn Rainey has always loved to tell stories and help others understand. As such, she is a published author and educator. But she is also the caregiver of her mother, an herb and vegetable gardener, cat wrangler, and crochet artist. She manages **ShelteringTree.Earth, LLC Publishing** and facilitates the **United Methodist Temple Prayer Shawl Ministry.**

After 38 years in education, Evelyn retired after having earned degrees and certificates in Early Childhood Education, Elementary Education, Gifted Education, Integrated Middle School Curriculum, English for Speakers of Other Languages, and Journalism. She also taught all grade levels from Kindergarten through Adult and at many different facilities, including jails and teen pregnancy centers.

Evelyn has several books published including science fiction, fantasy, historical fiction, new age urban fantasy, metaphysical and visionary, pastoral handbooks, and children's books. She currently has a list of a dozen new projects she plans to have published over the next few years. She has facilitated writer groups (and continues to do so with afternoon and evening meetings and would love you to join them – see the **Events** page on **ShelteringTree.Earth**). She has been guest speaker and guest author at writer conferences and conventions throughout the southeast US.

Her love of teaching has expanded into videos for book trailers, crochet lessons, meditation series, Bible studies, as well as interviews and writing lessons. (See her YouTube channel **evelynrainey4780**.)

Unable to travel as long as she remains her mother's caregiver, Evelyn is still able to conduct interviews and conferences via phone and video communication (zoom, duo, etc.) She welcomes questions and comments from her readers but prefers to be contacted initially through the contact page on her website **EvelynRainey.com**.

Our books will help you feed His sheep.

We are an exclusive publishing house. We specialize in uplifting, inspirational, and positive adult, juvenile and young adult, fiction and nonfiction, including poetry, native histories and spiritual paths, sermons, lectio divina, and pastoral and rabbinical resources in English, French, Spanish, Indigenous languages, and tri- and bilingual versions.

Our readers, once they finish one of our books, will be able to get up and face the world wiser, stronger, centered, and with the assurance that we are not alone: we are all a part of the Sheltering Tree on Earth.

If you as a writer feel that same calling, please refer to

ShelteringTree.Earth

www.ingramcontent.com/pod-product-compliance
Lightning Source LLC
Chambersburg PA
CBHW060513090426
42735CB00011B/2202